MW00807617

BUDDY'S TATTOO SHOP

SINCE 1948

4 MARLBOROUGH ST.
NEWPORT, R.I.

BY MARILYN MOTT TOLLESON

Stillwater River
Publications

Buddy's Tattoo Shop
Copyright © 2023 Marilyn Mott Tolleson.
Produced and printed
by Stillwater River Publications.
All rights reserved. Written and produced in the
United States of America. This book may not be reproduced
or sold in any form without the expressed, written
permission of the author and publisher.
Visit our website at
www.StillwaterPress.com
for more information.
Library of Congress Control Number: 2023906294
Hardcover ISBN: 978-1-960505-21-7
Paperback ISBN: 978-1-960505-22-4
1 2 3 4 5 6 7 8 9 10
Written by Marilyn Mott Tolleson.
Published by Stillwater River Publications,
Pawtucket, RI, USA.

Names: Tolleson, Marilyn Mott, author.
Title: Buddy's Tattoo Shop / written by Marilyn Mott Tolleson. Description: First Stillwater
River Publications edition. | Pawtucket, RI, USA : Stillwater River Publications, [2023]
Identifiers: ISBN: 978-1-960505-21-7 (hardcover) | 978-1-960505-22-4 (paperback) | LCCN:
2023906294
Subjects: LCSH: Mott, Buddy. | Tattoo artists--Rhode Island--Newport--Biography. | Buddy's
Tattoo Shop--Anecdotes. | Tattooing--Pictorial works. | Tattooing--Rhode Island--
Newport-- Anecdotes. | Tattooing--Technique. | Newport (R.I.)--History--20th century. |
LCGFT: Illustrated works. | Biographies. | Anecdotes.
Classification: LCC: GT2346.U6 T65 2023 | DDC: 391.65097457--dc23

The views and opinions expressed in this book
are solely those of the author
and do not necessarily reflect the
views and opinions of the publisher.

Dedicated
to a great Dad,
teacher and co-worker
Carlton A. **"BUDDY"** Mott
1924-2014

A man who works with his hands is a laborer.
A man who works with his head and his hands is a craftsman.
A man who works with his head, his hands and his heart is an artist.

St. Francis of Assisi

Most visits to a tattoo shop do leave a lasting impression and I'm not just talking about the permanent ink. Thank you to all who made my journey working with my Dad and sister Carolyn Mott Jaques never dull. In the pages ahead I'd like to share some of our entertaining shop stories that we jotted down over the many years, tattoo tips, the how to, a little business advice and some trade secrets.

- A few of the names have been changed to protect the guilty.

TABLE OF WHAT-NOT

"Hi, I'm nervous" said a customer.
"Hi, I'm Buddy."

Buddy had one of those personalities that made you feel welcomed. We made it a point to acknowledge everyone that walked in or even poked their head in the shop. He said to me, "I don't care what you say, just say something." Customers would tell us they had gone into other shops and felt ignored. Buddy would break the ice with many girls saying, "Are you here for the battleship on your chest?"

One girl said, "**NO**! I'm here for a destroyer on my shoulder" and that's what she got, well just the ship part pictured below.

By the way that's only Sharpie marker on his Hawaiian calendar. There wasn't much he didn't draw on.

Buddy always took extreme pride in his tattoo work. The advice Dad gave me just as I was starting my 1st tattoo was, "Put it on like you're wearing it."

Buddy was 56 when I started working with him in 1980. That is about the age when people start to look forward to retirement, NOT him. I spent almost 30 years tattooing with my father Buddy Mott. Dad outlined and I did the color. Everyone left with the 'Buddy's Tattoo' they came for. Buddy tattooed from 1948 to 2007, almost sixty years working a job he truly loved. In Dad's opinion, a tattooer was better than being a barber because a barber had to stand up while he worked. On average we tattooed about 3000 people per year. Multiply that by Buddy's 59 years and that's 177,000 tattoos, give or take. To put that into perspective the Civic Center here in Rhode Island holds about 17,000 seats. Picture filling that arena 10 ½ times and just shaking hands with each person. Now picture tattooing each one! I'm only good for about 80,000 or 4 ½ arenas.

ADVERTISING:

Buddy had thousands of people advertising for him all over the world. The sailors that came thru the large port of Newport RI were then shipped out in every direction.

A guy came in to the shop in the late 1960's and said, "Buddy, I'm not here for a tattoo, I just had to meet you. I heard all about you at a bar in Saigon."

In the early 1990's we got a picture and a note in the mail. Our bumper sticker:

BUDDY'S TATTOO SHOP
KEEPING AMERICA BEAUTIFUL
NEWPORT, RI

was on a US tank in Iraq. Buddy loved seeing that! He spent 3 years as a young man serving across Europe on a tank in World War II.

Buddy's early business cards had the address of the shop and no phone number.

This was the sign in the window. Navy time for 6 p.m. Buddy worked 6 nights a week. He took Sunday off and when asked if he would come in on a Sunday he would say, "I wouldn't tattoo the Pope on a Sunday."

Buddy made some new cards in the mid/late 70's and included our **home phone number!**

(No listing for the shop and yes there were a few calls at 2 a.m.) The new cards & a small sign in the window said call between 4 – 5p.m. to make an appointment.

An "appointment" only meant you would get a tattoo that night. We would take a handful of names and do them in the order that they showed up, starting at 7p.m. (Summertime we would start at 6 p.m.). It generally worked pretty good. There was the occasional gasp into the phone thinking we were expecting them at 7 in the morning! Customers before this were traveling 1-2+ hours to then find out we were booked solid for the night. We would round the corner and see up to 18

people standing in front of the small shop. They were all well aware of what group arrived first and they knew at some point that night they would get their tattoo. Some customers would tell us they got our phone number by calling the Newport Chamber of Commerce! They gave out our home phone number as it was shown in the shop window and directions to the shop. Very nice of them, we weren't even members! I finally convinced Dad in 1984-ish to get a shop phone. Neither of us were getting any younger. I'm only 5 feet tall (well my license says 5 feet). The phone company had introduced 911 for an emergency call number. It is better be safe than sorry... after much convincing he put a landline in the shop. Cell phones at that time were only for the wrist of Dick Tracey and the shoe of Maxwell Smart.

One night a very tall girl passed out COLD in the back room with me as I was coloring her tattoo. That was unusual. Seemed like if a customer was going to pass out it was in the first few minutes during the outline. Dad came running in. We laid her down on the floor being careful of her head and elevated her legs to help get the blood back to her head quicker. Buddy then stood over her with his hands around her back trying to work her lungs up and down. (For a large person he would grab their belt buckle area to work the lungs). Nothing! The smelling salts only made her eyes water. We glanced briefly at one another ready to grab the newly installed phone. At that very moment she came too. She said, "Oh sorry, I pass out all the time." Later that night as we were closing up Buddy said, "That girl scared me." I said, "Me too." He then said, "I thought we were going to have to call five eleven." I said, "Do me a favor, if I'm ever laying on the floor DON'T CALL FIVE ELEVEN, **IT'S 911 !!!**"

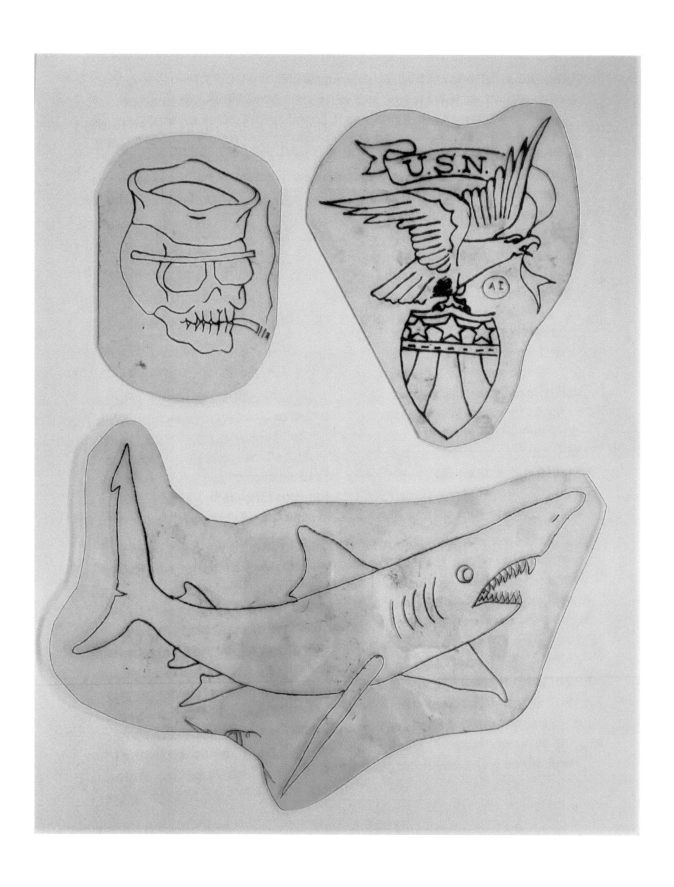

THE PHONE BOOK:

What's a phone book? It was a big, fat book, free from the telephone company. That's all that was available. No Google, Siri, My Space... The phone book for businesses was yellow aka "Yellow Pages." There was no option to pay a few more bucks and have your listing come up first...it was all by the alphabet. No surprise some of the shops in our area all happen to start with the letter A. We had Anchor Steam, Accupicture, Artistic Tattooing...

Love the name A Dash of Color. His name is A. (Alan) Dean Ash. A bad idea would be to put an A in front of Sin on Skin...or Troubled Soul...

BUSINESS CARDS:

There are printers more than capable to print you a box of 500 cards for a few

bucks. Buddy was friendly with a guy who owned a local art supply shop. They sold him the Black Pelican Drawing Ink for outlining the tattoos. This guy had an old, complete Kelsey Printing Press. Dad bought it and the countless drawers of type for $100 bucks in about 1965. He then taught

himself how to use it! It took hours to set up the type. One letter at a time, backwards and spaced to perfection in a carrier called a chase. The blank cards were placed one at a time in the holder, pushing hard to move the rollers over the disk with the ink on it until the press was fully closed. The release was no less effort. Take that card out and put in another. Two colored cards meant

doing all this twice, at 2 separate times for 1 card. My sister and I were probably 7 and 9 years old then. "I need another box of cards" he would frequently say as he was leaving for the shop. My sister Carolyn and I walked around like POPEYE, 1 arm bigger and more muscular than the other.

8

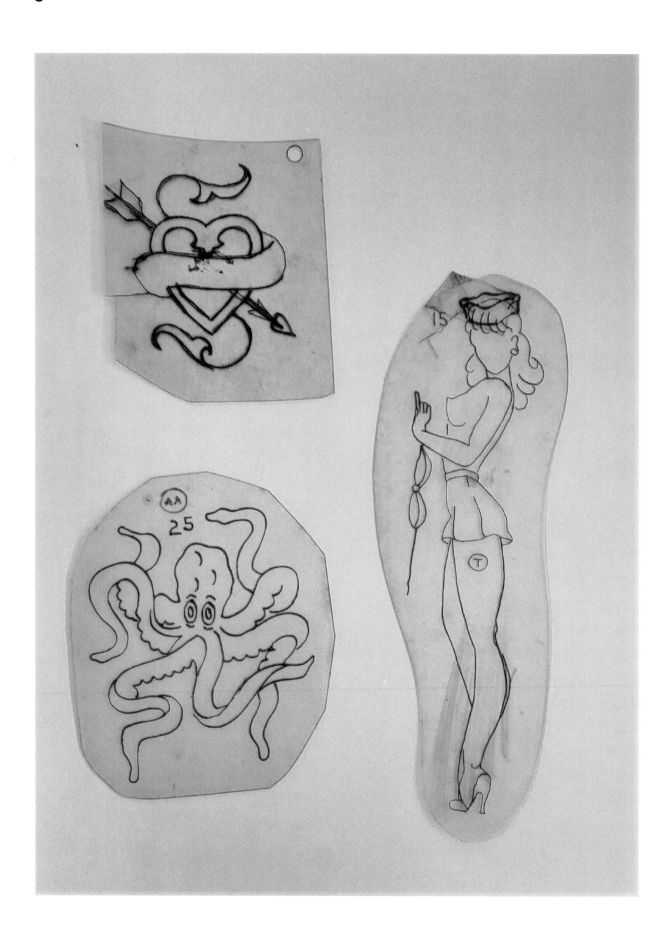

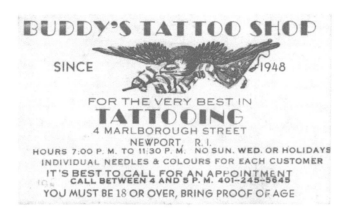

Including something fun on the card would hopefully make a person take more than one and share them. We also had besides our info, these numbers listed on the front of the card. 1 2 3 4 When you said, "Pick a number from 1 to 4" the only number not said was 3 and the majority of people picked 3. The back read "ALL SEX MANIACS PICK 3." There was also a saying

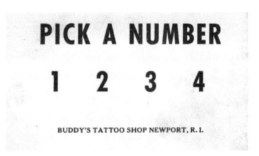

that when half was covered read a bit different.

IF YOU GOT DRUNK OLE BOY
A LITTLE AND STAGGERED
LAST NIGHT, DON'T FEEL BAD
SMILE   SMILE   SMILE

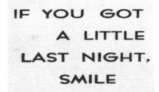

In the 60's Buddy would also give out little black books. That's what they were called "a little black book." Sailors or any customers would keep addresses and phone numbers, secret or otherwise, of special people. It was small to carry and hide easily. Eventually personalized match books became the most popular hand out.

This is one of my favorite cards from Buddy's collection.

Folded and opened.

1978 Tatowierungen   Herbert Hoffmann,   Hamburg, Germany

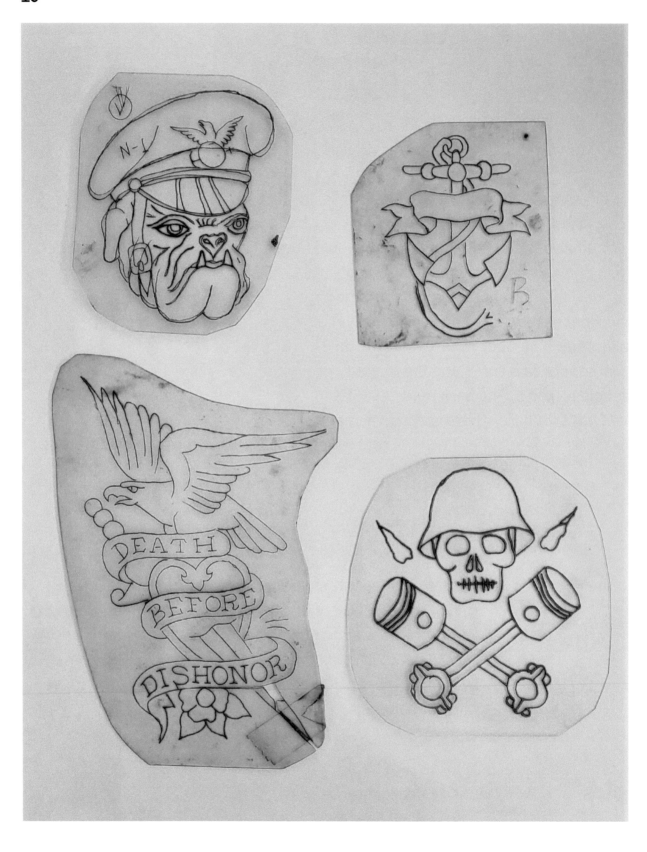

LOCATION:

Where the shop was located in our area made a big difference. Newport is actually an island connected with large bridges. It is at the far end driving from Massachusetts. Most of our business came from Fall River, New Bedford, south of Boston and Cape Cod. As more shops opened in almost every town in Rhode Island over the years the closer a shop was to the Massachusetts border meant more potential for business. Sin on Skin was on the State line. The "Welcome to Massachusetts" sign was less than 6 feet from his door. Tattooing was banned in Mass. in the 60's and reopened in 1999 /2000.

HANDLING PROBLEMS FROM WITHIN:

Back in the day (1960's) Cops would walk the beat. Buddy said he knew pretty much all of them. They would pop in the shop on a cold night to warm up. One cop would come in regularly and close his eyes for a little nap. Buddy would set a timer to wake him up at a certain time so he could check in at the call box. The cops would also tap on the window with their night stick as they walked by, like saying Hi. One night the cop tapped a little too hard and the window cracked. The Cop immediately yelled, "STOP THAT SAILOR!"

Fast forward to the 80's and we didn't know the cops. They were in squad cars by this point. The police station was diagonally across the street but calling the cops was not an option. If we made a call, it could be held against us at the yearly January Newport City Council meeting to renew our tattoo license.

What happened in the shop was dealt with in the shop and looking back we somehow were able to handle it. If shit started, we threatened to go home. Some customers had driven 2 or 3 hours to get in line to be tattooed. That statement of us going home got everybody's attention. There was usually a guy in the shop bigger than the guy causing the problem and problem over... Thankfully we were never held up. I always felt gypped being small, but when I was also signing in customers and playing bouncer it actually came in handy! I said to only a few "What are you going to do hit me?" That would be like taking a swing at your little sister. Some did carry guns... A guy wanted a tattoo on his chest and Dad said, "I'll have to charge you double if I have to go thru that shirt." Guy pulls the shirt off and ooops he's got a gun tucked in the front of his pants. Says, "Sorry" and transfers it to the waistline in the back. No pressure, the customer I was about to color, that we knew nothing about, except that he had a couple/few beers in him and a loaded gun down his pants!

EARLY FAMILY HISTORY:

Buddy was born in Bristol, RI, on October 25, 1924 as Carlton A. Mott. Bristol in the early to mid-1900's was a small, beautiful, coastal New England milling and boat building town. Carlton started school in the public schools and at the end of grade 2 the teacher said to my Grandmother that he was no trouble. He puts his head down the desk after lunch and takes a nap. His Mom yanked him out of there and took him over to the Catholic school to see what they could do with him and she wanted him to start over again! He would say, "I was the only kid in the 3rd grade with my own car." At 15 he was doing well in school but wasn't bringing any work home. My Grandma interpretated this as him not caring about school and sent him to get a full-time factory job the next day. Buddy had good grades, drew all over his books (no surprise) and had done all his homework in school during free period, so he could have his afternoons free, being with his friends fishing and having fun. Next, he was drafted into the Army months after the attack on Pearl Harbor.

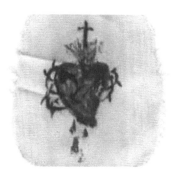

Emily (his Mom), a short lady, wasn't intimidated by hard work or projects. The house they lived in was built in 1792. (That's 17 years before Abe Lincoln was born! She re-wallpapered the dining room at 82. When Carlton asked her what she wanted for her 80th birthday, he said, "Name it and it's yours." She said, "A new wheelbarrow.") Emily also was a good artist. She painted Sacred Hearts on small pieces of white silk and gave one to her son and all his friends to keep in their pockets as they were being shipped out. Buddy starting his training at Fort Dix in New Jersey. His Unit went on to California for training in the desert. The military dentist said Carlton's teeth didn't meet in the back. They insisted he stay behind for necessary dental work. His 1st Platoon shipped out for Europe to join forces in WWII and 90 percent of that group were killed. Dad never had great teeth but after that he said he didn't mind. He believed his teeth saved his life. His new outfit was the 807th Tank Destroyer Battalion under General Patton's 3rd Army. Carlton's job on the tank was to load the cannon. Most of these guys were from the south. Patton made them fight wearing a tie! He hated that. Dad would say to us over the years, "If something happens to me don't bury me with a tie on!" (We didn't. He passed away November 2014. We chose: A Buddy's Tattoo T-shirt and hat, a navy-blue suit coat jacket with an American flag pin on the lapel and a pencil in his hand).

Some of the guys in his troop were unable to read or write. Carlton would write

the letters home for his fellow soldiers, to sweethearts or Moms, adding a butterfly or a red rose drawing on the letter. The red, when they could get it, was from cherry juice. His fellow soldiers appreciated him writing for them, and who wouldn't like some artwork. He also was taught how to play a small accordion by a German girl. Either he learned very quickly or he had many lessons with her because he played very well, entertaining the guys with a song every now and then. When they got shelled, after determining everyone was ok, the Commander would ask over the loud speaker "How's Mott's souvenirs?" They were sent home on leave and next were going to Japan when the war ended.

His Mother, seeing his ½ a dozen tattoos, told him to go into the bathroom and wash those things off. He pointed out the heart with MOM and all was well. Recently my nephew wanted a traditional heart and MOM tattoo. I looked thru the old flash and was surprised by all the MOM & DAD. Then I remembered him telling me his Dad seemed disappointed he wasn't included, so when it came time for him to draw his own flash he made most of them with both Mom & Dad. Buddy also had a full sailing ship tattooed on his chest. He said, "It hurt like hell! I went first, then my 3 buddies. There was no way I could show it hurt right on that bone or they never would have gotten one." After his own experience Buddy went easy on the customers getting middle of the chest tattoos. Carlton didn't have much of a Military rate but did his assigned duties and was honorably discharged. Buddy joined the Navy Reserve when he got out of the Army because he said, "If there was another war, I didn't want to sleep in the mud anymore." The next war was Korea. Since he didn't have much of a rate, they never called him! He said he felt a little guilty waving goodbye to his friends heading off to another war. Some of the guys were married with young children. He was 26, single, tattooing and driving a Caddy. Years later an honorable discharge came in the mail from the Navy. He had Army tattoos and that same night he tattooed U.S.N. on his inner wrist. Customers would ask, "You were in the Navy?" They were surprised with the answer:

"I was in both the Army and the Navy, why be half safe."

WE WERE NOT:

One of those state of the art, cool, eccentric shops.

We didn't have live tigers in the shop like Roy Boy from Indiana. We didn't have a live tattooed pig living in the store window (animal rights shut that down in the early 60's).

We didn't visit the dentist to have our teeth lengthened for the perfect vampire look. (That guy did look the part but had to re-learn how to speak again without the lisp.) His wife had the bite marks tattooed on her neck.

We didn't do social experiments like Spider Webb in the 70's convincing 10 people to get a tattoo of random time from a digital clock. The 10 were then invited to a NYC gallery to be exhibited. He had also tattooed an X on 999 people and gathered them for the tattooing of the 1000th X, a single large X, filled with 999 x's. No doubt another very interesting evening at an art gallery and tattooing was still outlawed. Spider called tattooing "warm art", 98.6° is pretty warm. Sadly, Spider passed away July 2022. I have a poster Spider signed to Buddy. It reads, *"All the best! Always - Your Fan- Spider Webb."* To see that Spider Webb signed it <u>Your Fan</u>, to my Dad, begins to show how much Buddy was respected.

Buddy kept in touch with various artists from around the world the old fashion way, writing letters and sending postcards. We made our own simple Christmas cards. (Hand painted banners or Sharpie Markers and White Out.)

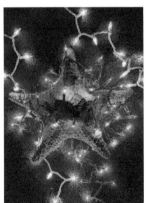

Unlike the Christmas card Buddy got in the mail in the early 1970's from Lyle Tuttle. This picture gives you an idea of what he was wearing besides his fully tattooed self. Worth a quick Google Search: Lyle Tuttle Christmas Lights. Oh you'll know it when you see it.

My favorite holiday memory in the shop (besides roasting chestnuts in the gas heater) is when a guy came in about two weeks before Christmas (early 80's) looked around and asked if we had any Christmas trees. He said his wife had given him 60 bucks and told him to come back with a Christmas tree. We tattooed on his outer calf a nicely decorated Douglas Fir complete with a tree skirt and wrapped presents under it.

In 1978 Buddy attended this Tattoo Convention in Amsterdam:

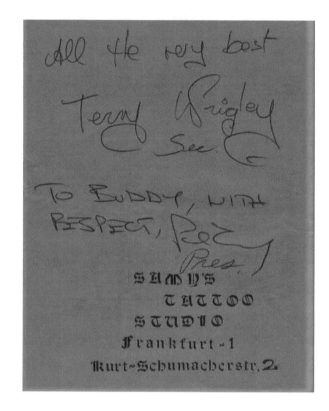

1979 Tattoo Artist Terry Wrigley asked fellow artists for help:

THE DESIGNS FROM CELL TWO FIFTY

IDEAL

THESE DESIGNS WERE NOT DRAWN UNDER/NORMAL CONDITIONS.THEY WERE NOT DRAWN
UNDER EVEN NORMAL CONDITIONS.THE ARTIST HAD NO DRAWING BOARD
NO RULER NO EARASER   AND NOTHING TO SHARPEN HIS PENCILS WITH EXCEPT
TO RUB THEM DOWN ON THE STONE FLOOR OF HIS SOLITARY CELL AT THE
INFAMOUS St GILLES PRISON. BELGIUM.

DURING THE PERIOD OF NEARLY ONE YEAR THAT THE ARTIST WORKED ON THESE DESIGNS
HE HEARD HARDLY ANY WORDS OF HIS MOTHER TOUNGE.HE WAS LOCKED AWAY IN
SOLITARY CONFINEMENT.AT TIMES HE WASNT ALLOWED A CHAIR. AT OTHERS
NO MIRROR .SOMETIMES HE WENT FOR WEEKS WITH OUT BEING ALLOWED TO TAKE A
SHOWER. AND FOR WHY????WHAT CRIME HAD THIS BROTHER ARTIST COMMITTED?
NONE   HE WAS ARRESTED VERY SHORTLY AFTER ATTENDING THE INTERNATION TATTOO
CONVENTION HELD IN AMSTERDAM HOLLAND IN MARCH 1978.

HOMEWARD BOUND HE WAS SIGHTSEEING IN BELGIUM WHEN HE WAS PICKED UP BY
THE POLICE AND ACCUSSED OF SERIOUS OFFENCES TO DO WITH A DRUG RING

IN ALL THE TIME HE WAS HELD IN SOLITARY CONFINEMENT HE PROTESTED HIS
INNOCENCE AND IN ALL THAT TIME NO ONE LISTENED TO HIM.YET WHEN AFTER NEARLY
A YEAR OF INHUMAN TREATMENT HE WAS FINALLY FREED NO ONE SAID
WE ARE SORRY.NO ONE SAID WE MADE A MISTAKE.NO ONE SAID WE REGRET THE
WAY YOU WERE TREATED.JUST GO

WHEN YOU WERE ASKED TO DONATE TO A SET OF THESE DESIGNS YOU WERE TOLD
THEY WERENT DRAWN UNDER IDEAL CONDITIONS.I WANT YOU TO LOOK AT THE DESIGNS ON
PAGES 7.8.9.10.11.12 &13.THESE DESIGNS WERE DRAWN WHEN BILLY PHILLIPS
HAD NOT EATEN FOR TEN DAYS.IN PROTEST AT THE TREATMENT GIVEN OUT TO HIM
HE WENT ON HUNGER STRIKE.

YET TO HELP HIS FAMILY BACK HOME IN AUSTRALIA HE DREW DESIGNS TO TRY TO
RAISE SOME MONEY TO HELP THEM. ONE TIME HE COMPLETTED A SET OF DESIGNS
AND ASKED THE PRISONERS DIRECTOR TO MAIL THEM TO ME SO THAT I COULD
SELL THEM TO YOU AND SEND THE CASH TO HIS WIFE AND FAMILY.THIS REQUEST WAS
REBUSED.HE WAS TOLD PRISONERS ARENT ALLOWED TO TAKE PART IN MONEY MAKING
SCHEMES. AND THE DESIGNS HE HAD SPENT HOURS OVER IN HIS SOLITARY CELL
WERE TAKEN FROM HIM.THE DESIGNS YOU SEE HERE ARE A SECOND SET HE DREW UP AND
WHICH WERE SMUGGLED OUT OF THE PRISON A PAGE AT A TIME SOMETIMES GLUED BETWEEN
THE PAGES OF LETTERS SENT TO FRIENDS ON THE OUTSIDE WHO MAILED THEM ON
TO ME SO THAT I COULD PUT A SET OF DESIGNS TOGETHER TO HELP HIS FAMILY.

BY THE TIME ALL THE DESIGNS HAD REACHED ME BILL PHILLIPS WAS FREED.BUT HIS
DETERMINATION TO NOT BUCKLE UNDER IMPRESSED ME GREATLY ALTHOUGH NOW BACK
HOME THINGS CANT BE TOO GOOD FOR HIM.HE HAS BEEN AWAY FROM HIS BUSINESS
FOR SO LONG THAT OTHER ARTISTS HAVE MOVED INTO THE AREA. HIS REGULAR
CLIENTS ARENT AWARE THAT HE HAS RETURNED AND THINGS CANT BE EASY FOR HIM.

I THOUGHT THAT WE HIS BROTHER ARTISTS SHOULD HELP BILL IN SOME SMALL WAY
AND I ALSO THOUGHT THAT YOU WOULD LIKE TO SHARE SOME OF THESE DESIGNS
I DOUBT IF EVER AGAIN A SET OF TATTOO DESIGNS WILL BE PRODUCED UNDER
SUCH CONDITIONS THEY ARE A TRIBUTE TO A BROTHER ARTISTS FORTITUDE
AND I AM SURE THAT IN TIME TO COME THEY WILL RANK ALONG SIDE THE
DRAWINGS OF RONALD SEARLE ANOTHER BRAVE MAN WHO DREW SECRETLY
WHILST SPENDING TIME IN A FOREIGN JAIL

PAGE TWO

TO MANY A YOUNG ARTIST SITTING AT HOME IN COMFORT USING EVERY
MODERN AID IN DRAWING THESE DESIGNS WILL COME IM SURE AS AN
INSPERATION.WHEN YOU CANT JUST GET THE SWING OF AN EAGLES FEET
JUST RIGHT AND YOU KEEP RUBBING IT OUT AND TRYING AGAIN AND AGAIN
AND AGAIN.DONT THROW YOUR PENCIL DOWN IN TEMPER AND SAY.....
ILL NEVER GET IT RIGHT! THINK OF A BROTHER ARTIST WHO SAT ON
THE STONE FLOOR OF A PRISON CELL WITH AN EMPTY BELLY AND DREW A SET
OF DESIGNS FROM MEMORY.

ON BEHALF OF BILLY PHILLIPS I THANK YOU FOR DONATION TOWARDS THESE
DESIGNS.THE CASH RAISED BY THESE DONATIONS WILL BE HANDED TO HIM
NOT IN THE NAME OF THE E.T.A.A. OF WHICH I AM THE SECRETARY.
BUT IN THE NAME OF BROTHER ARTISTS EVERYWHERE WHO HAVE SHOWN
THAT IN THIS STRANGE OLD WORLD OF OURS WE DO CARE FOR A BROTHER
ARTIST.
THANK YOU....
TERRY WRIGLEY. GLASGOW.1979.

BILL PHILLIPS   ST. GILLES

BILL PHILLIPS   ST GILLES

VISIT BELGIUM
FOR THE HOLIDAY OF A
LIFETIME

Our NO FRILLS shop was on purpose. The waiting area had no furniture except "the bench." Almost every one smoked. Buddy didn't want to take the chance of a lit cigarette slipping down between cushions and setting the place on fire. The beat up house we were attached to was rented to a family with 5

kids. Our store front was only about 12 feet wide, consisting of an 8-foot window and an entry door. Buddy told me there used to be 2 wooden benches, the second being along the front window. Buddy spoke of the night around a Navy pay day, with plenty of sailors in the shop, they all heard squealing tires and CRASH! A car instead of making a left, lost control and spun around smashing thru the shop window. He couldn't believe there were no sailors sitting on that bench at that time. He replaced the window, not the bench.

Customers sat on an old kitchen chair recovered in green vinyl. If you were getting a tattoo on the side of your hip, we had 3 of these chairs and you put your feet up on the shelf. Tattoo on the front of the hip or lower stomach area we had my childhood high chair. All the comforts of home...NOT.

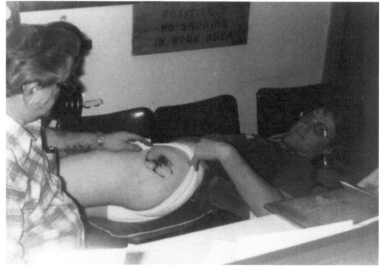

Buddy put a metal bar between the 2 front legs of the customers chair about 10" off the floor. He would put his foot on the bar and have the customer rest his arm across his knee, covered by a lap cloth. We NEVER let anyone straddle the chair. That was way too much lifting if a customer passed out in that position to slide the chair out. If the customer's ears were turning white or the color was draining from their face or if they asked for a glass of water, he would use the bar across the chair legs to push the chair back and take the guy's head and bring it towards the floor, lower than the heart, all in 1 motion to avoid them passing out.

We'd put a cold cloth on the back of the neck and have them sit a minute. They were usually sweating at this point. Then we would have them bring their head up slowly. Buddy would hand them a paper towel to "Dry your kisser." Only then they got the cup water. Rarely we would have to go lay them on the bench (unpadded wood) for a rest. Only one night that I remember running out of bench and chairs for them to all recover on. No doubt a full moon. If a guy starting to feel light headed and asked to go to the bathroom we made him do the head down instead. One night a tall, well built, State Police guy was getting tattooed. He looked a little pale and said he was going use the bathroom. I first asked him to just sit a minute. He stood and headed toward the bathroom. (Who am I to say no to a Statie?) He passed out only a few feet away near the bathroom door. When he came to, seconds later, he looked embarrassed. I'm glad he didn't get hurt. Turns out years later I found out he knew my husband. Small world for sure when we first made the connection! We now have a running joke that I wouldn't recognize him unless he was pale and laying on the floor.

Some guys we laid on the floor while passed out, would come to seeing people (us) standing above them. Not remembering where they were, some figured maybe they were in a fight and cold cocked...they woke up swinging, fists clenched! The first thing we would do is remind them that they are at the tattoo shop... The most important thing you can do as a person is passing out is PROTECT THEIR HEAD. A few people while just watching would pass out. I looked up one night and saw a very pale gal holding a 1-year-old baby. I walked over to her and took hold of the kid as she rather gracefully headed for the floor.

I didn't have a foot rest bar on the chair. I put my foot on a gallon paint can. The cover was shiny from constant use. I have no idea what color was in that can. This raised my apron covered knee high enough to put the customers arm across to work on. Eventually Buddy designed and made an adjustable arm rest rig. One for me too! We only used the can 1 other time when a guy wanted a Harley Eagle tattooed on the top of his head with the talons coming down on his forehead. He sat on the can so I could color it as I was standing! Not much meat on the top of the head, felt like I was chipping cement. Making small talk with that customer he tells me his daughter is getting married soon in a Catholic Church and his ex-wife wants to know what he plans on doing with his head for the wedding (no hats on men in Church). He told her, he plans on bringing it! This is a big world, lots of churches everywhere and he says the name of the church. It is where my son goes to school! I asked him if they questioned the tattoo leave my name out of it.

ID'S:

We had to focus on age. The sign right under the wall of flash: YOU MUST BE 18 (for many years it was 21). We would tell kids just shy of their 18th birthday come back right after your birthday and we'll give you a break in price. Lots did. Some states passed a law if you got caught tattooing a minor you could be charged with child abuse or MUTILITION OF A MINOR. No thanks. But many will tell you "I was 17…, shit faced…" Makes for a better story.

A young looking 17 year old customer said with a straight face one night, "They put the wrong year on my Military ID. I'm really 18. That is supposed to say 1975 not 1976. Don't you hate that!" He said he was going to call President Clinton and complain. Buddy chimed in, "Let me know what he says."

A guy came in with his daughter and she had a phony looking Virginia license. The Dad pulls up his sleeve and he has a tattoo with the matching name and birth date.

Young looking guy has his birth certificate for an ID. I asked him, "What's your mother's name?" He said, "Mom."

1984 A guy calls, "If I'm 18 and you can tell I'm 18 do I still need and ID?" My answer is "YES". I asked, "When were you born?" He said, "1967." I told him you're not 18. He yells, "Ma what year was I born?" A voice from the background yells, "66 stupid."

Always had a few comedians in the shop especially on the sign in cards:
Proof of age: Wrinkles
In the 1970's occupation was a question!
Occupation: STUD (in capital letters)!
Female customer for occupation wrote: "Housewife".
Location of tattoo (meaning where on your body it was going) guy writes:
Newport. Over the years the sign in cards had gotten longer and longer. Ron Dario, one of the few artists that Buddy taught, went to a lawyer when he was opening his own shop and let us use a copy. It started: I ____(Name)____ being of sound mind and body…!!!   HA (Make sure to include a paragraph giving you permission to use customers photos taken at the shop for advertising, display, a book or social media.)

I remember the I first time I handed a guy a sign in card to start to fill out (because I was super busy) and he only made an X on the bottom. Took me a minute but then I took the card back and filled it out for him. He was a nice guy and pretty well spoken but couldn't read or write. He came in several times after that and one night told me he was planning a trip to New Hampshire. A few weeks later I ask him how his trip was. Well, his friend cancelled last minute so he couldn't go. He confided he wouldn't be able to read the signs.

GETTING STARTED AND THE NAME "BUDDY":

Back from the War, Carlton's Mom encouraged her son to get married so he would settle down. The marriage lasted 6 months. If you add up all the factory jobs, house painting jobs, shingling, roofing etc., Carlton had 22 jobs before tattooing. He said about getting started, "I borrowed a few bucks from Ma and sent for my first tattoo kit.

It came from Jenson in Long Beach, California." He also may have sent away for some info from Popular Mechanics and then I found the typed How To Tattoo from Northeast Tattoo Supply in Portland Maine. When asked, "When did you become a tattoo artist?" Answer: "When I ran out of friends to work on."

Carlton growing up was nicknamed TT as in MoTT. In addition to his full-time day job, he started tattooing in a local bar in his small hometown. Guys would say, 'Hey Bud, can I get a __tattoo?' On the flip side he referred to many male customers, if he didn't know their names, as Skip. ...and there you have it, how he got to be known as Buddy.

He, Buddy, used his older brother's roller skate box and made a portable set up to

work the bars. He painted some sample tattoos on a bed sheet and would thumb

tack the designs on a nearby wall. Business was pretty good, complete with a bullet to bite on if anybody asked. If a fight broke out he just closed the cover of the box, pulled the sheet off the wall, rolled it up, tucked it under his arm and out the door he went before the cops showed up.

He admitted he was nervous when the first woman (an older woman) asked for a tattoo. "She wanted a small rose. As soon as I started her jaw dropped. She didn't expect it to sting so much and her dentures landed in my lap."

In the mid 1970's Buddy was attending an Army reunion in California. He went to Jenson's shop and got to meet him. He figured it must be his son but it was him! The guy he was working on, turns out Dad tattooed the guy's brother while he was in the Navy stationed in Newport!

Buddy's first shop was in Newport, Rhode Island, opened in 1951. As the story goes his brother- in- law was pinning up the pictures on the wall and the sailors were already walking in. The day job he had at the time was paying him $1.25 an hour.

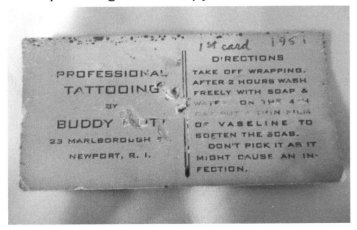

The 1st hour tattooing he made 11 bucks, (names were only 50 cents back then). Shortly after that he quit his day job! The shop was open nights and he couldn't believe he had the whole day off. He, never a morning person, actually enjoyed literally throwing his alarm clock out the window.

Flash (designs) were all hand drawn. First you sketched a handful of outlines to useable sizes on heavy parchment type paper. Next using the side of a pencil, you

would blacken the back of the paper where the designs were. That was your 'carbon paper'. Trace over again pushing hard onto a thicker paper. It was enough to see a faint outline. Now trace over all the designs with black ink, shade and color the designs. We're not done yet, acetate stencils to transfer the designs onto the skin still had to be traced over with an engraver or by hand with the tip of a sharpened playing dart. Over time tattoo artists would cut the popular designs out of the flash pages and stick them on another cardboard. Eventually a simple frame with glass helped preserve the drawings but you would still have to put tape around the back of the frame to prevent the cigarette smoke from getting into the pictures.

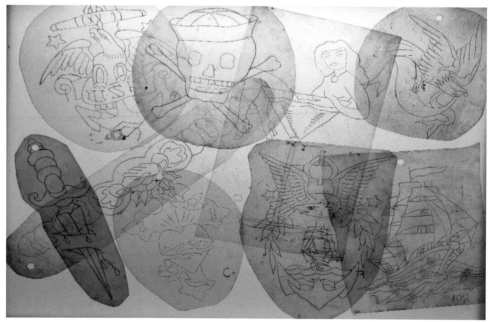

He also sent away $5. to Milton Zeis for a bag of old acetate stencils and more how to tips. The stencils were worn but worth it.

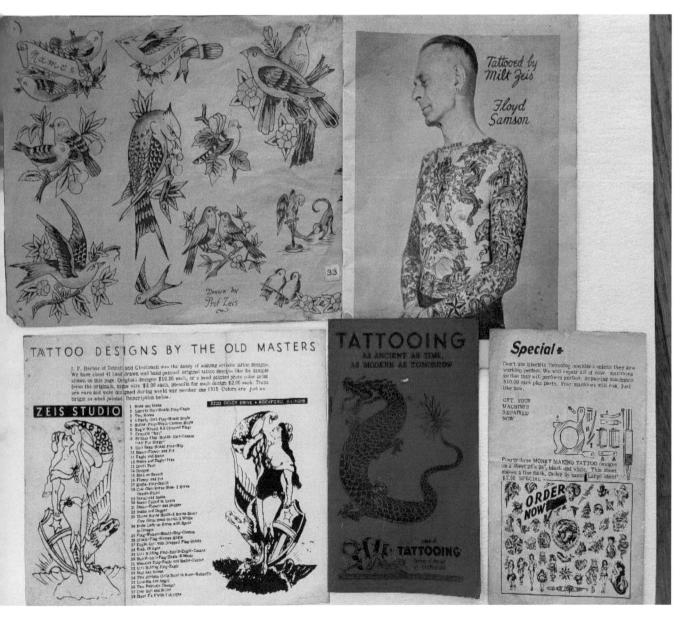

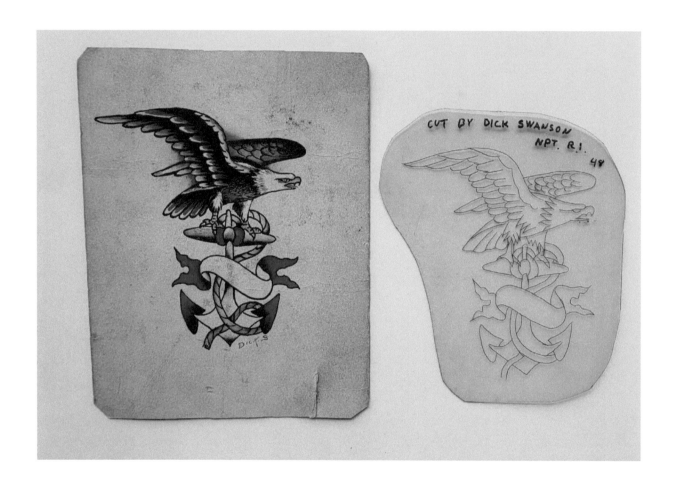

"Prof. Milt. Zeis" must have been quite a character. "Uncle Milty" written on the bottom of the card, evidently was also a clown that could be hired to perform a magic trick at any occasion… This card has a 1965 calendar on the back.

These drawings were done by Sailor Rox for his friend Dick Swanson. Sailor Rox tattooed in the 40's. Dick Swanson followed and then had Fred Day work with him. Buddy started with Fred in the early 1950's. Buddy ended up with a few of Dick and Fred's old drawings and stencils. I couldn't believe that I found the cut out of the rose and the flash page from Sailor Rox to Dick dated 1947!

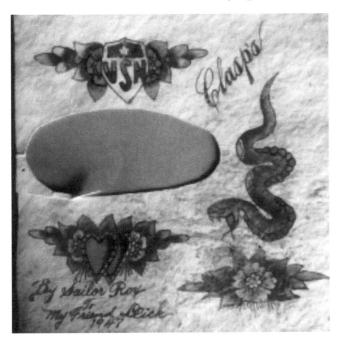

Some of the drawings by Dick Swanson, complete with heavy tracing paper and acetate stencils were on loan in February 2022 to the American Swedish Historical Museum in Philadelphia. They were doing an exhibit on tattoo artists of Swedish descent titled TATTOO THRU IDENTITY. It was an honor to be able to contribute to the show in Buddy's name and a good excuse to go on a road trip to Philly.

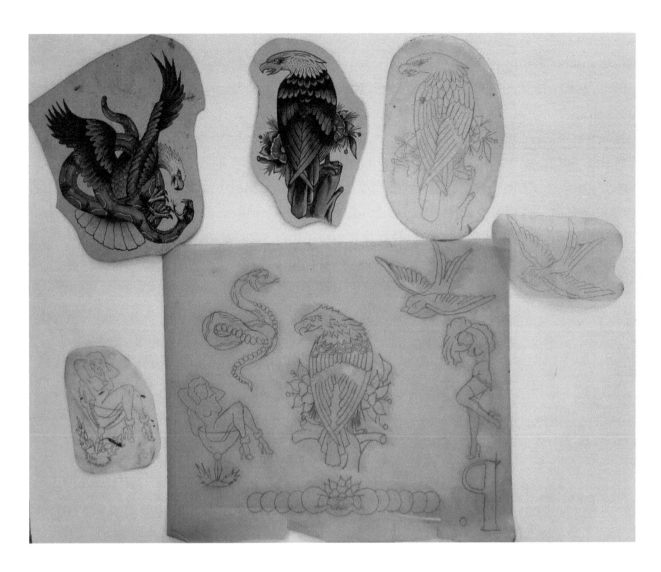

The exhibit continued thru Valentine's Day. Seemed fitting to include the romantic devil and gal!

HOW DAD MET MOM:

Buddy was 28 when he met my Mother. She was 34! Never married and her name was Madonna, actually Bertha Madonna Emin. She was the oldest of five girls. If she was a boy she would have been a Junior – but she was a girl. My Grandfather Leander insisted that my Grandmother name the baby after herself, Bertha. Mom was born in 1918, the end of World War I and "Big Bertha" was a large gun! Her Mother not wanting to be known as that made Mom's official name Bertha Madonna but they would call her Madonna. Her folks were very strict. In sharp contrast to Dad's early elementary school experiences, my

Grandmother who was a school teacher had my mother start school in 3rd grade at age 5 and as a result she graduated college at 18! Madonna then started working as a school music teacher in her hometown of Smithfield, RI. She also worked as a Catholic Church organist since she was 12! Back in those days school teachers were most always spinsters, never to be married. One of Mom's friends got engaged and was fired. The school department would not chance a married teacher standing in front of a class pregnant. Mom was a graduate of R.I.C.E (RI College of Education, now RIC) and then trained in Boston. She was a member of the "Who's Who in Music" and once played Carnegie Hall. She would also play the State Fairs in Massachusetts

and New York on some weekends and during the summer. She towed her Hammond B3 organ by herself in an open trailer with an electric tail gate to the shows. A few years ago in 2015, after both Mom and Dad had passed, my sister and I were cleaning out their house to sell and we came across a Vaudeville poster in the attic. It was advertising Madonna at the Organ complete with live animal acts! We realized only then that with Mom's Vaudeville and Dad's Tattooing backgrounds WE CAME FROM CARNIE FOLK!

Mom also rarely, but occasionally, played in local night clubs. She decided to re-evaluate her life at age 34 and decided she wanted a family. One night Buddy stopped in after work to see his friend the bartender. With taps on the heels of his boots he clicked his way across the floor with 2 requests: One for a song and the other to join him after closing for a coffee. The rest is history! They were married 61 years. Of all the places the newlyweds could have gone for a honeymoon, they jumped in the car and headed for the Indy 500. By the time they got there it was time to head back.

Mom's Mother, when first hearing about the younger man she met, (Mom was 6 years older than Dad) wasn't thrilled about her choice. He had tattoos, rode a motorcycle, only completed his 1st year of high school, was divorced and tattooed for a living! In the mid 1960's both of my parents had lost their Dads. Business

was good and my Father paid for us all, including their Mothers, to go on a trip to see 6 Capitals in Europe including Rome and Paris.

"Big" Bertha (pictured on my Mother's right) became a fan of my Dad during the trip.

My Mom was NOT a traditional gambler. She never bought a scratch ticket or put a quarter into a slot machine. She decided to invest (gamble) all the money they would have paid over the years for family health insurance into the stock market. She was very lucky, just one broken bone each and paid cash. When Dad was 64 and had gained a bunch of weight, I asked/begged her to please get him health insurance for 1 year until he would be eligible for Medicare. I pointed out she had beaten the system. She finally agreed, and he did have some minor medical complications that year.

WHERE WERE BUDDY'S EARLY SHOPS LOCATED? GOOD QUESTION! He talked about having 5 shops in Newport in a 4 block area…Looking thru many old shop licenses and trying to make heads or tails with the cross outs and changes written in pen by the City of Newport on City issued certificates wasn't easy.

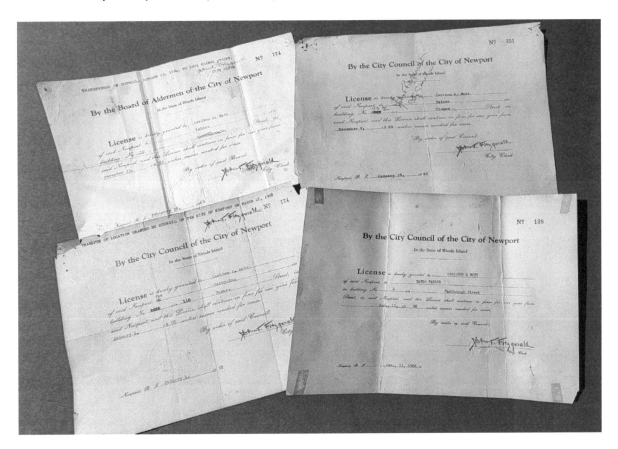

This is what I came up with:

The address of 23 Marlborough St. was Buddy's first shop address in Newport, 1951-53. The very same afternoon in 1953, 6 months after Buddy & Madonna were married, as they were signing mortgage papers for a house, the Navy was pinning a 'CLOSED UNTIL FURTHER NOTICE' document on all 3 of the Newport tattoo shops doors! A sailor had come down with Hepatitis. The shops were closed for months. I do not know if the cause was ever determined. After a few months of doing any and everything to pay that new mortgage in 1953 Buddy opened a shop in Fall River, Massachusetts, where he worked for a few months. Buddy's next Newport license is from 1954. The address written again in pen by the City Solicitor transfers Buddy's tattoo license to a new location, 100 ½ Thames Street.

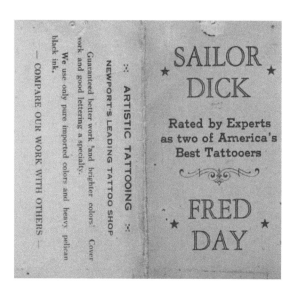

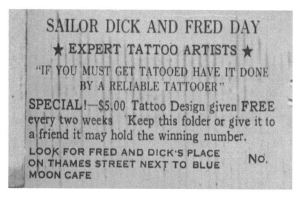

Well, on the card it says Sailor Dick and Fred Day, 107 ½ Thames St. next to Blue Moon Cafe. (The second zero on number 100 ½ maybe should have been a 7?)

PROPER CARE OF TATTOOES

Soak bandage with water and remove in two hours.—Leave bandage off. Keep tattoo clean. Apply vaseline or olive oil after five or six days to ease shedding of scabs.—AND DON'T PICK IT!

IF YOU WANT IT DONE RIGHT, HAVE IT PUT ON AT FRED AND DICK'S PLACE
107½ Thames Street, Newport, R. I.

Long time Tattoo Artist Sailor Dick Swanson retired and his business partner Fred Day had been working alone for the last few years. Fred contacted Buddy and offered him a job to come back to Newport and work with him.

The shop was next to the most popular strip joint in the heart of Navy Newport, The Blue Moon. Thames Street was commonly referred to as "Blood Alley", the seedy section of the city, full of

watering holes, fistfights and the unpleasant smells of puke and piss. There were plenty of sailors on shore leave with a few bucks to spend especially after pay day.

RI Photograph Collection, Providence Public Library. Thames St. Looking West Down Northam Lane. Wilfred Warren Photographer, 1966

Fred, also a sign painter taught Buddy the ins and outs of lettering. They painted an occasional sign, the specials for the restaurant across the street and ALL the banners for the "coming attractions" at that well known strip club. (Very neighborly). Fred said sign painting was "Something to fall back on if tattooing folded up again."

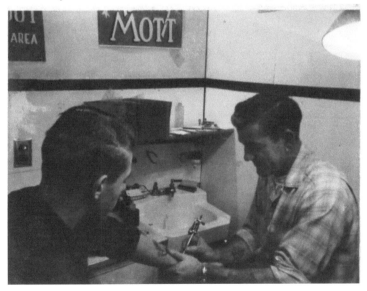

They realized when they were out of work the number of things big and small that were taken for granted.

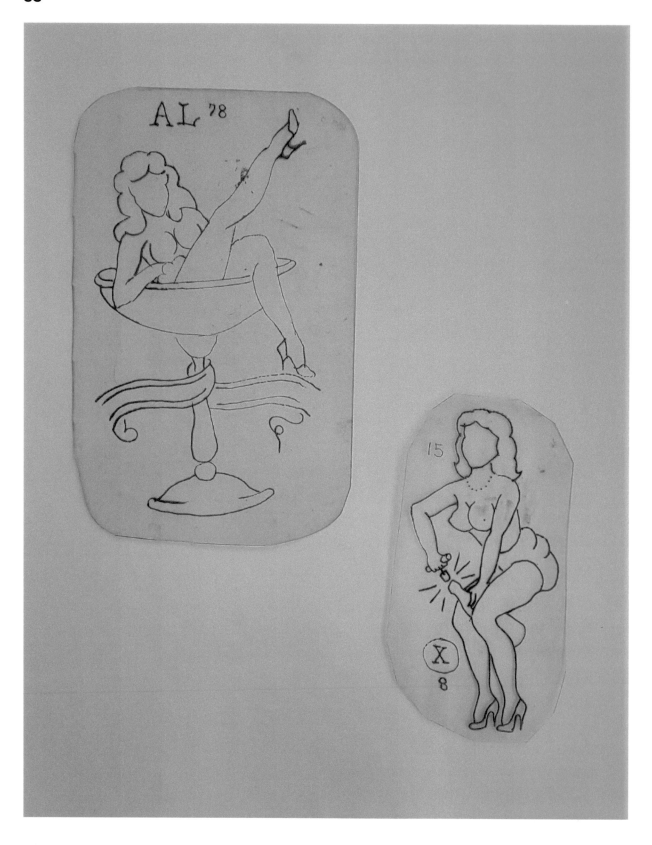

Buddy also told me the juke box was right on the other side of the wall and sometimes the bass would just about rattle the flash in frames off their walls. Over the next seven years they worked together. At least 20 times over the years Fred would say he was going to get out of the business and sell Buddy the shop. Fred's patience was wearing thin with the exception of house cats. He loved them, even strays. Buddy told me Fred owned so many cats the curtains in his house were just threads from the window sills down. Fred would let a random cat sleep in the shop on cold nights. He referred to all the shop cats as Maggie and would say, "Good night Maggie" as he was closing the door to lock up, whether or not a stray was spending the night in there.

One night a sailor was being an ass and Fred opened the door and threw him by the shirt sleeve and belt, out into the street. He didn't bother to look to see if a car was coming. Luckily there wasn't! Finally, he did sell the shop to Buddy. A few months later Fred said he wanted back in. Buddy was happy working alone and told him he would help him set up new shop of his own. A year or so later Fred's new shop went up in flames because of a fire next door. Fred retired after that.

 Buddy's other addresses were 110 Thames St. in the late 50's (another blue ink on the City License Certificate). Next was 113 ½ Thames St. from 1960 to 1965. 113 ½ was next to Sam's Locker. These were shops open 24 hours a day so a sailor

could if he wanted, bring his civilian clothes with him and change there and later return to the ship back in uniform. Buddy was paid a few hundred dollars to relocate to 113 ½ . The city was in the midst of rejuvenating or put another way, knocking down and rebuilding sections. 4 Marlborough St. was his longest rental from 1966 to 2005.

Buddy recalled after moving out of one of the shops the old one was struck by lightning 3 days later. The Hurricane of 1954 left almost all of the businesses downtown under at least a couple of feet of salt water from the surge. Then what? Sweep the water out, mop up, do some minor repairs, wait for the electricity to come back on and reopen.
FACT: NO one was going to insure a tattoo business!

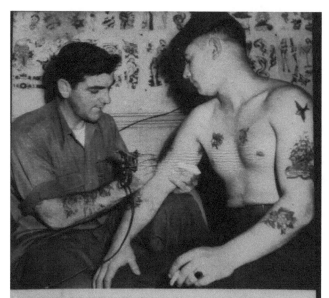

IN MILITARY CIRCLES the tatooer is sought out for special effects in appearance. Buddy Mott of Newport is needling Pfc. Jack Holloway of the Newport Marine Barracks.

There were laws on the books in Newport from 1945 amended in 1953 to add a new chapter entitled "An Ordinance to License and Regulate Tattooing and Tattooing Establishments" added to the City of Newport Ordinance No. 101 of the Representative Council. Tattooing was prohibited without a license obtained from the City of Newport. The Police Chief had to ok that you were of good moral character... It then lists A thru H that I found very interesting, especially their order of importance.

a) No person under the influence of intoxicating liquor shall be tattooed.

b) **No female shall be tattooed.**

c) No tattooing work shall be done on the hands, feet, face or private parts. (Quoting that made our life easier).

d) No person under 21 years of age shall be tattooed and proof of age required.

e) A record shall be kept of all customers. If a civilian name and address. Military shall include name, serial number and ship or station of service personnel. Records must be kept on hand.

f) No tattooing establishment shall remain open later than 1am.

g) No person shall be tattooed more often than once in any one week, nor in any case until any prior work has completely healed.

h) New needles shall be installed **daily** (OMG) and machine tubes must be placed in boiling water before use. Color dyes shall be kept in white glass jars with plastic tops and kept clean. All tubes shall have stainless steel points.

1957 Fred and Buddy were asked to attend a meeting with Navy Chiefs of Staff to give their input about updating regulations. The meeting went well and it seemed like smooth sailing from there.

October 10, 1961 a newspaper article states that 6 NY tattoo parlors were briefly shut down in 1959 with concerns of spreading Hepatitis. Norfolk, VA was shut down in 1958. It went on to say that as of November 1, 1961 all tattooing in New York would be banned. The article continued referring to the death of a young boy after being tattooed. NY authorities claimed they traced 32 deaths of hepatitis and 1 death to a tattoo parlor in the past 3 years. On December 7th of 1961 according to an article in the Providence Journal the Health Commissioner of Newport proposed not closing but not renewing tattoo parlor licenses as they became due that year. Sounds like the same thing to me. (Buddy's license was due in January!) Dr. Ciarla, the Superintendent of Health at the time said tattooing was a health menace that could not be properly regulated. There was talk of suspending all licenses for the 3 Newport shops that night. It was decided to hold off for one week letting the shops continue to operate during that week. The following week on Dec. 14th the Health Commissioner gave the board 1 week to draft strict controls. The vote was 3 to 1 in favor of imposing strict new regulations. Dr. Rogers opposed based on reports that 30 deaths from Serum Hepatitis were traced to a New York tattoo parlor. (??? Depends on which article you read and who they were quoting). States were closing all around Rhode Island. New York shutting down was the final straw for Massachusetts figuring many tattooers would move across the border. Scully Square in Boston, home of the Liberty family tattoo businesses was demolished and The Government Center was built.

The Health Commissioner agreed in 1961 to make the shops install and use autoclaves for sterilizing needles and use individual colors for each customer. He was quoted in various newspaper articles that the added expenses would probably (he was hoping) drive the shops out of business. There were also serious recommendations coming from the State House in 1962 House Bill No. 1118 to limit tattooing to doctors only. Grasping at straws Buddy called his brother-in - law, an OBGYN Doctor to ask if we would spend some time in the shop if it came to that. The law never passed. Thank you Dr. Paul Blackmore for considering.

 Shop licenses in the City were capped and somehow Newport and the State were not shut down. Looking back the rest of the 1960's into the 70's, 80's - even thru the 90's there was a Northeast monopoly taking place in Rhode Island that no one could have ever imagined. Massachusetts didn't start tattooing again until 2000!

We, the Newport tattooers of the 1980's (Buddy, myself, Ruby and her co-worker Bret Lohnes) were the only 4 artists in the 2 tattoo shops in the state that had to go for a physical every year. I don't know when that started, pre 1980 for sure. Ruby Wolfe was the wife of Don LeBlanc owner of Sailor Don's and the Trawler Restaurant. When he retired, she ran the business as Tattoos by Ruby. Captain Bret has remained tattooing in Newport, owner/operator of Celtic Tattoo. The Newport City Council in 1986 removed the cap on shops adding one on Collins St. to Hobo. He stayed a couple of years and moved back up north. We convinced Ron Dario (one of the 5 people to be taught by Buddy, 2 being me and my sister) to take over the shop. Perfect, he was always off on an adventure and was hardly ever open. In 1990 as tattoo shops started opening in almost every town across the state, towns were asking the Health Dept. for guidance. The RI Department of Health then started an annual renewal license and a yearly inspection of shops. The Health Dept. contacted us and a couple of the other shops and came to see us for an informal lesson on tattooing. They wanted to know what was involved in giving and caring for a tattoo. How do we keep records of who we worked on etc. We kept it simple. We didn't say all an inspector would have to do is say especially these days with all the regs is, "Let me see your trash." We as a state became licensed and inspected. (Newport still did their annual City Council review but we didn't have to get any more letters, like before, from our Doctor stating we didn't have anything 'catchy').

All the tattooers in the state were asked to attend a briefing in Providence at the Dept. of Health, (1991). The race began in typical Rhode Island fashion with the obsession for the lowest numbers. Example: Cars with low numbers on license plates were highly sort after. If you had one either you 'knew a guy', bought it from someone or it was passed down thru the family. Over the years it became illegal to transfer a license plate to a non-family member. Buddy is proudly showing off his license plate **807**. (WWII Tank Destroyer Battalion). Mom & Dad also had CM 31 & MM 31 plates. The first new RI tattoo license was issued to Dean Ash, Number 1 and his brother Rusty who taught him was number 2. That didn't go over well and they had them switched. Buddy was 11 and I am 12. I wished they distributed them by years in business. Doesn't make much sense that number 11 taught number 1. Now the numbers are into the thousands.

TIMES IN NEWPORT WERE CHANGIN':

The news reported in the early 1970's that the Navy was abruptly being pulled out of Newport. I remember the look on Dad's face when he told my Mother. It was a 'we may never eat again' look. The Rhode Island native, former Governor, now Secretary of the Navy did this! At the nationally known Bristol, RI 4th of July parade when John Chaffee came walking by, Buddy wouldn't even shake his hand.

BUT Long haired hippie type…The navy

pulls out right as the "long haired hippie type" (Dad's words), flower children of the 60's & 70's and motorcycle riders all wanted to get tattooed! If a guy was getting a pot leaf on his forearm he would suggest another spot saying, "Just because you smoke it, doesn't mean you have to advertise it." Buddy couldn't believe business was better than ever. The Navy only got paid the 15th and the 30TH of every month. (Those two dates and about 3-4 days after that, he was very busy. A few times he drove home as the sun was coming up!)

The new clientele kept him busy every night! Business was great! The photo is from 1971, taken by © Martha Cooper and published in the Total Tattoo Book.

Buddy's traditional wall of flash always remained as it was. Many guys still wanted to get a traditional tattoo or one like their Dad's had. He also started offering more popular designs of the times. (Thank you, Martha, for giving me permission to use it here. I have had many people gladly giving me permission to use pictures and share the enthusiasm for me writing Buddy's stories.)

44

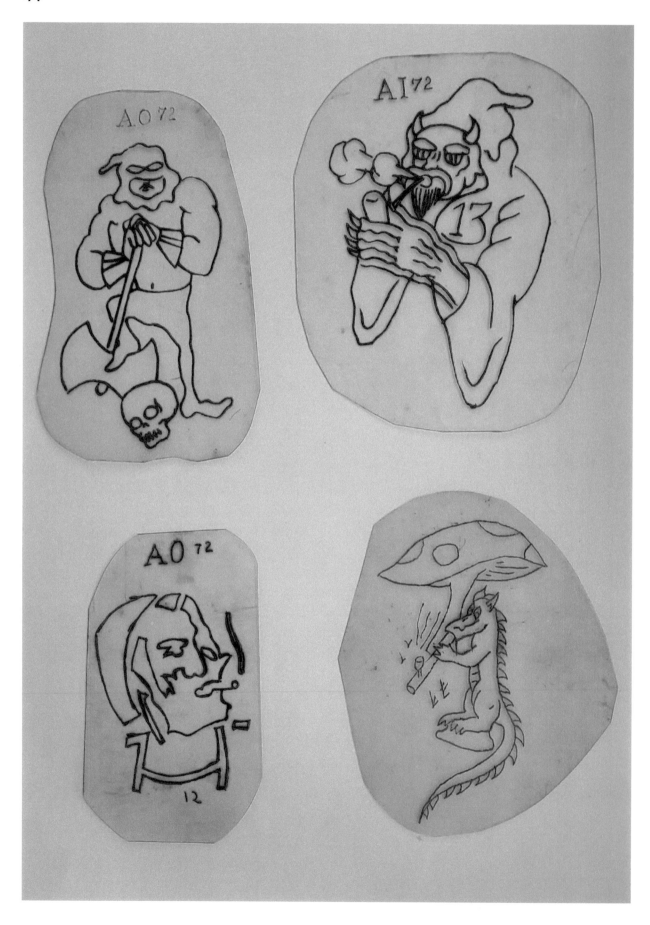

Buddy was asked a few times by customers waiting and watching for hours if he sold stock! He intentionally had only $5 and $10 bills in the wallet he pulled out to make change. The payment money went in his back pants pocket. Some guys after watching one after another get tattooed and pay would ask, "Do you make money at this?" Dad would say, "Enough to put gas in the Mercedes and steak on the table. I MEAN - gas in the Volkswagen and hamburger on the table." (Mom & Dad had matching Mercedes.)

ENGRAVING:

Buddy was great at lettering be it hand painted, gold leaf signs, tattoos or

engraving. His lettering style was crisp and detailed with serfs and thick and thin letters with a drop shade. He made a rig to engrave Zippo lighters for Navy and civilians, placing the lighter into a recessed hole he hollowed out on a board. Much easier with your hand on the same level as the surface of the lighter.

46

1958

1965

FYI a **"RIG"** was on the idea of a gadget that he would come up with, for a specific purpose, made out of whatever was on hand at the time. Usually just a bit of fine tuning and they all worked great. Buddy was proud of his creations and there was no stopping him after he bought his first hot glue gun!

REMODELING:

When our family would go on vacation the sign in the window said, 'remodeling'. Never said, 'Closed for Vacation.' Buddy figured keep people guessing if we were in town or not, no need to announce it. Repeat customers would come in and remark the shop didn't look any different. Buddy would tell them, "I put a new ball in the toilet, or I changed the bulb in the shit house." When we did remodel the one time,

we didn't close! In 1980 when I started working with Buddy the walls were an ugly mint green Formica. It only took 4 or 5 years for me to convince him to put up paneling, install a drop ceiling, add 1 more exhaust fan to get rid of the smoke (he had quit smoking), put a sink in my work area (the back room) and let me tile over the cement floor. Oh, and lose the mason jars with the lids screwed to the bottom of the shelf. He was always a do it yourselfer. He could/should have hired a couple of guys...NO, he and I did it. (Have you figured out by now Buddy didn't have any sons!) Daily we would go in about 10 a.m. and rebuild til 4ish, put the tools away, clean the place up, go get a bite to eat and open for business that night. This went on for many weeks! A new McDonalds started to be built as we were starting our remodel. They were finished and open and we started eating there before our projects were complete. The night the sink in my back room was put in, but no time to hook up the drain that day, Buddy shoved a 5 gallon bucket under it and told me to hang something in front of it. The look on the guy's face as he heard the water going down the drain and splashing into the bucket was funny. He said, "That doesn't sound right" and offered to take a look. Nice guy. He shook his head when he saw the bucket.

Buddy would take it upon himself to fix whatever was broken and never bothered the landlord. The rent was mailed every month. Only once we had to shut the power off and Buddy said to me, "Kill the main." I unscrewed all the glass fuses. The air conditioner never shut off!!! (Making the rent even more of a bargain). In 1966 when Buddy moved into 4 Marlborough St. the rent was $35 a month.

In 1977 a registered letter was sent from the landlord S. Spiratos. He informed Buddy in writing the rent was going up to $45 per month. I give up researching these addresses, FACT: 40 years at 4 Marlborough St. Recently I came across the letter from the landlord referring to number 4 as 6 Marlborough!

One afternoon in the early 1980's while we were banging nails for our remodel, a gray haired, small woman with an English accent opened the door slightly and Buddy asked, "Can I help you?" "I'm the landlord", she said. "I've never been in here." The rent then jumped to $165 a month. She was the widow of S. Spiratos. Her Greek husband and his brothers owned many business properties in Newport. Most were made up of several connected small store fronts with living spaces above. During the downtown area rejuvenation project of the 1960's shops of all kinds were paid to move a few blocks away from the center of the City. I believe 4 out of the 5 shops he rented were with the same brothers as landlords. The last Newport move, in 1966, consisted of a handful of sailors carrying the stuff down the street a couple of blocks, to the new location. It was another old barber shop, long and narrow. Turns out, we saw in about 2010, after the shop was knocked down, behind where the wall of flash hung was the side of the house next door complete with shingles and 2 windows that were covered all those years. Buddy tried many times to buy the building but it was tangled up in an estate. Parking became impossible after resident Parking Sticker Required signs went up all around the shop. The last thing we did leaving this rental property was throw the key in the mail slot. It dawned on me years later that the older English lady probably didn't have a key! If possible, try and buy the building you work in. You're not going to throw yourself out and property values generally go up.

THE GREATEST JOB:

Buddy, before I joined him, had worked alone for many, many years. Everything he needed was within arm's reach. Save a step, make it an efficient use of time and time is money. He would time himself doing a variety of things. Competing with himself. I realized how long he was aware/obsessed with time when he told me the rather large ship, under full sail he had tattooed on his chest after basic training, was done in Philly by Professor Hoffe. It took 1 hour and 6 minutes and cost $15 bucks. He also loved the TV show The Magic of Oil Painting with Bill Alexander. (Bob Ross took over years later...happy clouds.) The idea of the show was to learn how to paint a complete oil landscape painting in a half hour. Dad practiced this new skill and got it down to 22 minutes. NEVER caring about seeing a TV celebrity, his phrase was, "I wouldn't cross the street to see that guy"... he heard

Bill Alexander was coming to New England for a book signing. He announced he was going and invited me along. We drove for a couple of hours and then my father stood patiently in a long line! Dad brought one of his tattoo photo albums. Bill thumbed through the variety of pictures including some of the tattoos on gals and said to him, "I want your job." Dad smiled all the way home.

WHEN I STARTED IN 1980:

I'll be the 1st to admit I had no idea what to expect working with my Dad at the shop. We were used to doing and creating some pretty neat stuff with him at home in the basement. We as kids (my sister and I) never went or got to hang out at the shop. I'd only read the articles written about him in the 60's and 70's. Once in a while 1 or more guys driving over the top, cool and loud bikes would pull into the driveway at our house. (To the best of my best recollections my mother never rode on the back of a bike). Dad was home during the daytime and after dinner off he went to Newport, 6 nights a week to work. I knew he was pretty well known. Once when I was in high school, I got to go to school late because he was on TV, a pre-taped segment of Good Morning America.

My 1st night we pulled up and customers were waiting out front. As we crossed the street it was like Moses parting the Red Sea. My cousin's husband Joe was with us too. He had been helping Buddy on weekends for a few years. He signed in customers, checked ID's and cleaned up. Buddy is about to unlock the door and says, "Step aside." He didn't want me or anyone else to get hit by the almost ½ inch steel bar that was across the door covering the key hole.

First, he undid the pad lock releasing the bar to swing down. It was heavy enough that you had to guide it and stop it before it took a hunk out of the corner of the doorway. In we go! Stinks like stale cigarettes. There was a dustpan with a long handle full of butts, swept up from the night before and left overnight to make sure they were out. The place was simple and very dated. Whatever his formula was it was working as customers followed us in. Next, he turned the heat up. It was cold, February in New England cold. I remember thinking the guy going first hopefully didn't have to take his shirt off. The heat came from an old free standing gas space heater that customers would also sit on (until it was red hot). Within minutes Buddy was tattooing the 1st customer. He always had a sense of humor and the best laugh. When customers would ask him, "Is this going to hurt?" His answer, "I won't feel a thing." He often referred to the shop as "the sore arm factory". I don't know if he was talking about the folks getting a tattoo or his arm after a long night's work.

THE PLACE LOOKED A LOT BETTER AT NIGHT!!!

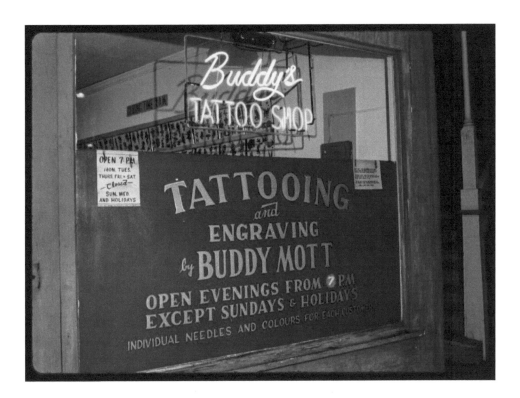

So, I survived night one. Coats on, lights off, make sure the toilet isn't running. He stood quiet and listened for a minute for any noises outside the door.

Over the years, MANY times it seemed like the amount of time we were delayed from leaving the shop, for whatever reason, was how far behind we were from some awful car accidents with bodies and beer cans across the road. Dad over his years had become a believer about life's sense of timing remembering how his bad teeth had saved him in the war. Another time while fighting overseas he had hitched a ride from a guy driving an Army jeep. An Officer with a hot attitude threw Buddy out and told him to start walking. A few hundred yards down the road a wire had been placed by the Germans across the road, tight, and about 4 feet off the ground. Jeeps had 2 metal poles sticking out of the hood to prevent getting caught up in these wires. This safety feature evidently was missing on this beat up jeep. The wire decapitated both the driver and Officer.

Finally, out we go. Buddy swings the metal bar into position over the keyhole. As he clicked the pad lock he said, "Good night Maggie." I didn't ask.

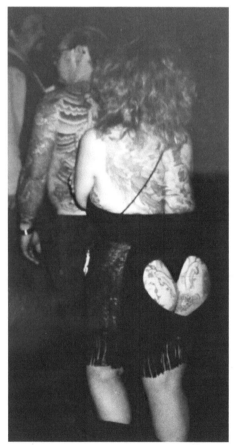

My first 6 months included: March 1980, one month into my new job we went to National's Tattoo Convention in Philly. It was all new to me. Some of the most famous talented artists, suppliers and fans were all in that room! I met Paul Rogers, Lyle, Ed Hardy, Grandpa Groovy, Huck Spaulding, Flo from National and the fully tattooed green man, to name a few. (I remembered seeing him in a Tattoo Magazine. To then see, in person, so much green starting at the top of his head was a lot to take in.) So, what does one wear to the banquet at a tat convention? I remember packing a pair of corduroy pants and my Frye boots. We're going down on the elevator and it stopped at a floor. The doors open and there is a lady with many tattoos, wearing a fancy dress with fringe on the bottom. I realize I'm underdressed! Oh well. She got in and then turned around. WOW! She had cut the ass cheeks out of the dress to better show off her tattoos!

I still had my full-time day job as a travel agent in Providence at Weiner Travel and also taught group ice skating classes. The owner, an older Jewish woman, wanted me to answer the phone, "Weiner Travel, as in hot dog." I quit when she was talking about giving me a raise. (Minimum wage was going up from $3. to $3.25).

I always figured Dad was an honest guy. Over the years when illegal or questionable 'opportunities' presented themselves at the shop, he didn't bite. I knew he was well known, enjoyed his job, and was successful. He knew he was in the right place at the right time and was thankful. As kids when Mom showed us how to use the sewing machine, that was under the window on Dad's side of the bed, she would tell us constantly to make sure we didn't drop a pin on the rug. Ok! I got it! I wouldn't want to step on a pin either...one day she said, "Check again. When your father kneels down to say his prayers, he better not kneel on a pin..." What? Every night she told us he would kneel down and thank God for his blessings. We never knew that until she said it. (Well he went to bed at 3 a.m.)

Summer 1980 and we are selling plenty of T-shirts. They had Buddy's signature sailing ship design and also included Newport, RI. Besides selling shirts to our customers more and more tourists were happy with one for a souvenir.

This was also the year of the popular America's Cup 12 Meter Sailing Races. Held every 3 years the best of the Americans would compete against the winner of the foreign entrants. This contest is over 130 years old. Every night Dad would pick me up for work and hand me the appointment sheet. Written under the customers names it said Sports Illustrated. I asked why

he wrote that on the pad. I've never seen him buy one. He said, "They called me today and want to come take some pictures tonight." (Thanks for the heads up!) Sure enough, the door opened and in came a large camera crew. They wanted to include many different aspects of Newport – post Navy.

The caption in the August 1980 issue, written by Frank Deford read: "As befits a Navy town, Newport has a tattoo parlor, though customers aren't always old salts."

The article also referred to the old Thames Street as Blood Alley full of drunken sailors, fighting and blood. Newport, 1980, the new normal included tourists, boutiques and the 'Red pants crowd' as the writer categorized the yachting crowd. Rich red colored 'Brenton' pants that won't take a crease down the front, a non-ironed blue blazer and tan leather slip on boat shoes, NO socks.

The next night on the appointment sheet it said AP. I asked Dad, "What is AP?" He says, "Associated Press called. They're coming tonight." AGAIN, thanks Dad for the heads up! They wrote a great article. Dad said, "I think we should order more T-shirts." Two days later a journalist from the New York Times called and was not pleased that AP had beat her to it. She said, "I'm coming anyway", and she did.

MORE BOOKS, NEWSPAPER INTERVIEWS AND A MOVIE:

Every now and again a guy would come into the shop and buy a shirt and say he was making a documentary or movie etc.

One guy only told us he would like to take some pictures and hopefully one would make 'the book'. We were unaware it was for <u>A Day in the Life of America</u>.

200 professional photographers were sent out all over the country to take pictures for just 1 day, the 24 hour period of May 2nd 1986 . ©Michael O'Brien took pictures of nearly every customer in the shop. Months later we were sent a copy of the large book of photographs. His photo was chosen from the quarter of a million submitted. There is a stunning two page spread of one of our regular customers Paul Mello, showing his dragon tattoo. Paul was a nice, photogenic, marine electrician from New Bedford, MA. That night he wanted to have his girlfriend's name added "in Chinese." Buddy told him he didn't speak Chinese and sent him up the street to the Chinese restaurant and they wrote it down. We heard Paul passed away a short time after the publication.

America's Cup Race with all the fanfare is back in Newport, 1983. Reporter Sid Moody from the Associated Press started his piece with the words: If your beauty isn't skin deep there is always Buddy Mott. (That AP interview was syndicated and Dad's Army friends and fellow tattoo artists from all over the country sent us a copy.) That was the last year the sailboat race was hosted in Newport. The actual 24 mile sailing races are held so far off shore they are seen by very few. The excitement was just being in Newport during the races. The Australians won and took the Cup and the rights of being the hosting port with them for the next race. They credited themselves for the win by using their secret winged keel. Great lengths and speculation buzzed about what was hiding below the boat. Before the unveiling the keel was covered with a lead fabric to prevent someone potentially trying to x-ray it!.

Sid wrote there were once 7 Epidermal Etchers in Newport. He captured the feel of the shop and some of Buddy's remarks writing: Within minutes the waiting line included several women giggling like they're buying their 1st bra. Buddy reassured them pointing to the bottom of the pull-down shade that said: Privacy for the Ladies.

He claims he puts on dark glasses if his duties take him to a restricted area. A tattoo is a card laid and a card played. When it comes to spelling Buddy writes it down first. Buddy said, "If we make a mistake, we have to throw the arm away."

A movie maker bought a shirt one night. He felt the need to tell us he was going to be making a movie about sailing and the movie would be filmed in Newport. We thanked him for buying the shirt and wished him well. Three of my friends one night were talking about being extras in a sailing movie being filmed in Newport called: Wind. (My mother once participated as an extra in the movie Mr. North, also filmed in Newport, going day after day in the heat. She and many others ended up on the cutting room floor). Months later I get a call at work from my sailing friends. They had just gone to see the movie. In one scene they saw the back corner of one boat (for a split second) and another recognized her elbow.

WIND

Then as they kept watching, looking and hoping, the movie screen showed a whole scene with the lead actor wearing our Buddy's Tattoo tank top! They couldn't believe it!

'TV TECHNICIANS':

Most customers can tell you what was on TV when they got tattooed. Buddy had the direct view of the TV, the customer was watching thru a mirror behind Buddy. Watching Wheel of Fortune puzzles backwards in the mirror wasn't easy. One night there was a Dolly Parton Special. Dad was doing a tattoo of a woman on a guy's back. He must have been influenced by Dolly's figure because I've never seen him make boobs that big on a tattoo!

The 1st guy that brought his new Sony Walkman and headphones to listen to a cassette tape during the tattoo seemed like a good idea at the time. Within minutes he starts tapping his foot and movin' to the rock & roll. Sorry, no more Walkmans.

NEVER did we have cable at the shop. We watched the 3 major networks and would occasionally try to tune in a UHF channel. Buddy had put an outdoor roof antenna attached to the ceiling of the back room (my work area) with a pulley set up that looped right beside him at his work station so he didn't have to get up to adjust it, when he worked alone. When customers would ask why didn't we have a remote-controlled TV, he would say, "I do. Watch this. Will one of you TV technicians put that on Channel 6 for me?" The closest guy would reach up and turn the knob. Buddy would then say, "Thanks, what do I need a remote for, I 've got you guys!" Early cable was just 1 channel, only on at night and showed a movie (Preview TV). He didn't want to put that in the shop figuring if a group got into the movie, they would stick around to watch the end crowding up the waiting area.

Every night when Dad got home from work, he would sit in the kitchen and read while having have a couple of beers, and sharing the cheese and crackers with the 2 large, black Newfoundland dogs. One named **Cinder**ella and the other Hamilton (after the 20-dollar bill.) Buddy once read a complete set of encyclopedias, NEVER anything fiction. His favorites were National Geographic and anything about WWII and cannons. Buddy collected a full set of Nat'l Geographics, 1914-2012. One night settling in with a new book he saw it was a novel. It got thrown in the trash after he tore it in half. Questions on the Jeopardy TV show, especially about History and Geography, he would quickly and correctly answer (while tattooing too). He got insulted one night when a guy said, "This must be a repeat show."

GET RICH QUICK SCHEME:

BUDDY
5.24.82

NOT! We bought a 2nd hand upright Pac Man machine for the shop. After it was set up and ready to make money, we were told we would need to apply for a license to operate it in a business. Well, the City had recently passed some ordinances and we were within 500 feet of a Church and that was the end of that. Not 1 quarter was earned but it was funny seeing my Dad trying to play a video game.

THE HOW TO:

Yes, it's great to have a well running machine and a good eye and ability for art, but that is just the beginning. It's the dealing with customers with personalities (or lack of) from A to Z. "Ooops" is no longer in your vocabulary. The night a guy got the 2 birds on his chest and with no warning sneezed as Buddy was making the beak on bird # 2, leaving a one inch line heading down the guy's chest. Without saying a word Buddy went back to the 1st outlined bird and added the same line. He threw in a couple of green vine leaves, matched the other side and the guy was thrilled and couldn't believe that wasn't going to cost him extra.

THE WORK SPACE:

Customers stood at the glass and watched customers being tattooed, one after the other as they waited their turn. There was also a chain about waist high that continued across to the wall. This was to keep people away from the work area. We would let a (ONE) friend also duck under the chain and sit on the spare chair to watch. Not everything goes according to the plan. This girl said she needed some moral support.

Sorry about the quality of many of these photos. If it wasn't for the Polaroid camera we had at the shop, I wouldn't have as many memories to share.

EVERYONE IS DIFFERENT, DON'T EVER ASSUME

SKIN:

Our sign-in form had a question, "Do you have any tattoos now?" I glanced up at a customer and almost checked the NO box. I couldn't see his tattoos until he happened to turned slightly. He was covered! The color applied to all tattoos is the same but darker the customers skin the less visible they become. Very dark skin made it harder for us to see the design we were trying to tattoo.

 If a person gets 2 tattoos in the same night the area of the first one becomes numb to a degree. THIS HURTS was common to hear when we started the second.

Overworking a tattoo in one session leads to a longer healing time and a chance the dry skin may leave some spots in the color. Stop before it gets raw!

Do not cover a mole with a tattoo. When a mole changes shape or color that can be a sign of skin cancer. Suggest another area or tattoo around it.

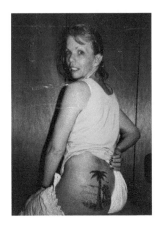

Older scars can be disguised with a tattoo. Jessie and I go way back. She wanted the large scar on her back side covered with a palm tree and a devil woman. She is a hoot. I saw her tie a double knot in a cherry stem at a wedding reception (she did take her teeth out first), and we all saw the tattoo that night too.

Make sure a scar is fully healed before you tattoo over it.

I used to think a sunburn was red skin. I learned it is blood coming to the surface to protect the skin. We refused a few customers with a bad sunburn because it would bleed like crazy as we were doing it. The loose peeling skin could/would clog the machine and the healing process is longer because the skin is torn up.

So, this job of tattooing isn't as glamourous as you may have thought.

Some guys would come in in the summer and say their tattoo looks faded. The color isn't as bright… Buddy asked some what they did for a job. They were so tan, mostly outside workers, especially roofers and fishermen. Ironically tattoos do look better and brighter in the winter when the tan had gone, but go figure, winter in New England and you're covered in long sleeved clothing.

There was a small sign on the wall behind Buddy that simply said, "Sit still and don't move." One night according to Dad's old notes, "A Hep Cat jumped into the straight razor." The cut it made was a fine line. Buddy taped it together with the scotch tape and suggested putting the tattoo on the other arm. He pointed to the sit still sign. A couple of years later the guy was back for more and asked Buddy if he remembered…there was barely a scar! I like the expression "Hep Cat". It was a different time some 40 to 50 years ago. Some of my notes start with, "a couple of gay guys come in…" In one of Dad's notes from the late 60's - early 70's it starts, "3 Queens". Took me a minute to realize he wasn't talking about playing cards.

SELF PREP:

"I shaved myself. Can I have a discount?"

Another guy: "Let me know ½ hour before it's my turn." He goes in the bathroom and rubbed a whole tube of Preparation H on the area we were going to tattoo! I found the empty tube on the bathroom. Gross! (another 80's expression)

Different night, guy asked for the same heads up. He went outside and drank lots of something and took a handful of ? It was almost his turn when we laid him on the bench and woke him up later so we could close up. He asked, "How'd my tattoo came out?"

THE MACHINE:

Buddy and Ronnie (from Providence) both spent years working on their own versions a rotary machine. Buddy became interested six months after I started working with him. He said my hand was so small he wanted to try something with less weight and that worked the same every night, regardless of temperature or humidity. Rotaries also didn't get hot from constant use. I remember him running the old machines under cold water to cool them.

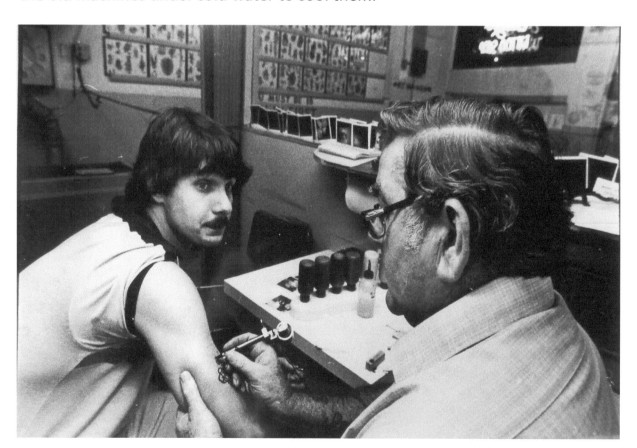

Previous to this every machine that Buddy bought, the 1st thing he did was cut away as much weight from the frame as he could. He never understood guys tattooing all night with big heavy tubes and heavy machines. He also cut all his tubes and needle bars shorter so the machine would ride resting against the index fingers upper knuckle. He glued a piece of leather to the frame for a cushion. The idea behind cutting back the tubes besides weight was the machine felt like an extension of your hand. He made me a small block of wood that would clamp on to the tube, about 1" wide. That was the difference between his hand and mine. I would take his machine he outlined the customer with and bring it and the customer in the back with me to finish the tattoo. Most tattooers use 2 machines, one for outlining and the other for shading.

Special Built Rotary
20 SEC needle change.
3.4 ozs.   Buddy Matt

Everybody we worked on loved the rotary. It didn't make that loud annoying buzzing sound. A fellow artist KJ from Providence got the rotary tattooed on his leg. Buddy thought that was great, and what a compliment for something he had worked so hard on!

Many years ago, by mistake, Buddy had put a shader tube in a standard coil machine with an outline needle. Needles are like metal paint brushes. Different sizes for different applications. Outline tubes have a small circular opening on the bottom like a pen. The shader tube has a rectangular bottom to hold

6 flat needles, generally used to shade and color a tattoo. Buddy decided to leave the shading tube in and turned it to a 45-degree angle to the right with machine facing him, putting the outline needle in the V of the shading tube. He couldn't believe how much ink that tube held! He could tattoo long steady lines without having to re-dip constantly. He got rid of the outline tubes. I have never tattooed with an outline tube. Some of the little motors in the rotary machines would give off a signal, just enough to make a couple of lines across the TV screen (pre-cable). Didn't bother us. When the machine was running, we weren't looking

62

at the TV. EXCEPT that 1 night when OJ Simpson was driving the white Bronco down the highway in the infamous Low Speed chase. It went on for almost 2 hours. I'd glance up at the TV every now and then, didn't want to miss anything. One time I looked over at my TV and I saw lines thru the picture. Took me a second to figure out what that could be. Only time I evidently was watching TV and running the machine at the same time!

What customers did know was that tattoo machines, connected to a power source, had a knob to adjust the amount of power to be used. This was mounted on the wall for all to see and marked from low to high. Some nights the electricity in the shop was stronger than others and shading needles needed just a little more juice because they are made up of more needles soldered together. What the customers didn't know was the knob running the controls was intentionally reversed. If you were acting like an ass he reached over and turned the knob down like he was being nice. Actually, it was being turned up! Yes, that would make the tattoo hurt more and would shut the guy up. Only a couple of times he turned it so far "down" I looked at him and rolled my eyes in disgust. (He also reversed the hot and cold in the bathroom sink. There were 2 faucets and people by habit, seem to reach for the hot. Clever- but that's an el cheapo move!)

The machine was connected to a foot switch like a sewing machine. Buddy wanted one with a lower profile so he made them out of hinges with springs and a contact point. Some customers would wonder how he was turning it on because of the foot switch was mostly hidden under his foot. One night Buddy made another rig and put the switch behind the cabinet door. All he had to do was press his foot to the right against the door. This really got people scratching their head. Well, the joke was on him. A couple of weeks later Buddy's hip was KILLING him. That was the end of that. My back room had a simple set up and a low-profile foot switch as well. Some customers thought they were funny when Buddy said to follow me into the back room...some would say, "Not the torture chamber!"... a guy one night looked at me with a non-trusting look on his face. He then asked how the machine turned on and as it was laying on the counter, I took my fingers and made a motion like a wizard over it and it started buzzing. He thought I was definitely a witch! We had a good laugh when I showed him.

MAKING NEEDLES:

In the late 1940's / early 50's it was common for a tattooer to have black ink tattooed in no particular pattern on the outer palm of the hand - just a little back and forth on the meat of the outer edge of the hand. When putting a new needle in the machine they would dip it in the black and test it on themselves first, seeing if it was running smooth. (Beyond gross!) I think Buddy was clever enough to adjust a machine without doing that. The skin on the palm does wear constantly and the black would eventually wear off.

Tattooers had to make their own needles. He came up with a way to make needles with almost no effort. (We didn't own a labor-intensive soldering iron!) New needles for every customer made our job easier. The tattoo looked better, bleeds less and heals faster. Over-used needles don't dull as you would think,

they hook. **THE SECRET** - the solder was melted in a small stainless-steel pot, like a jeweler, suspended over a butane torch. The needles were placed in a wooden jig he made and dipped. We tinned the bars the same way, dipping a few at a time. This part of the process was done a bit slower than attaching the needles to the bars. (Too much cold metal being inserted at once could blow some of the solder right out of the pot). Place a group of needles in the jig, one dip quickly in and out, run a wet Q-tip down the solder to smooth it, and voila, done! I made needles for people all over the country, Canada and one in Puerto Rico. Some would send me their bars to re-needle. I used the business name "Making Points" for mailing purposes. After the severe storm Hurricane Marilyn struck Puerto Rico in 1995, I never heard from that customer again, also named Marilyn.

 Daily Buddy would make our needles for the shop while having his 'morning' coffee. (11 a.m.) In every bag there were 2 needle bars (3 round and a 6 flat) and a tube. Buddy made an indent on the loop end of the outline bar so after he tore the bag in half he could see and feel which one was the outliner. (Save a step, instead of a 50/50 chance.)

COLOR:

Mixing color was the messiest job on the planet! We mixed the dry pigmented powder in a blender with READY FOR IT, DRUM ROLL **WITCH HAZEL**! That was one of the biggest, "Don't tell a living soul" things at the shop. Rubbing alcohol dried out the ink too fast. We mixed it to the consistency of tooth paste. If while mixing it was thick and you needed to add a little more liquid, when you took the cap off an air pocket lifted from the bottom to the top. It made a sound, BOOF.

Seemed like slow motion you couldn't stop, watching the cloud of unmixed dry pigment and everything around the area, including me, turn color. After I completed my 1st mixing job, I walked out from the back room and Buddy said, "What the hell happened to you?" Only then he told me to just slightly open the lid as you tap the bottom on the counter to release any air bubbles!!!!! Thanks Dad! I blew my nose blue for 2 days!!

There was also the "banana rig." he made. This wooden shaped banana with holes drilled about 1" deep spaced evenly apart held the colors in ink bottles

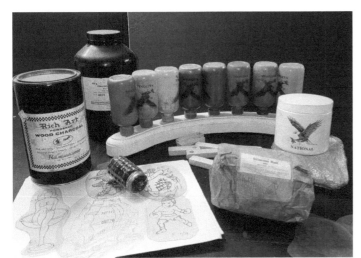

upside down. This position stopped the ink from drying in the caps and tips of the bottles. Some guys would put the color bottles laying sideways between 2 rollers to keep the ink moving.

TIP: Coloring tattoos; Always start with the darkest and finish with the yellows and whites.

These designs that he drew for his wall of flash, besides a black outline were colored only using red, yellow and green. Didn't matter if it was eyeshadow or water under a ship until the 80's, it was green. The day I suggested ordering dry powders to make pink and purple ink he looked at me like I was crazy.

66

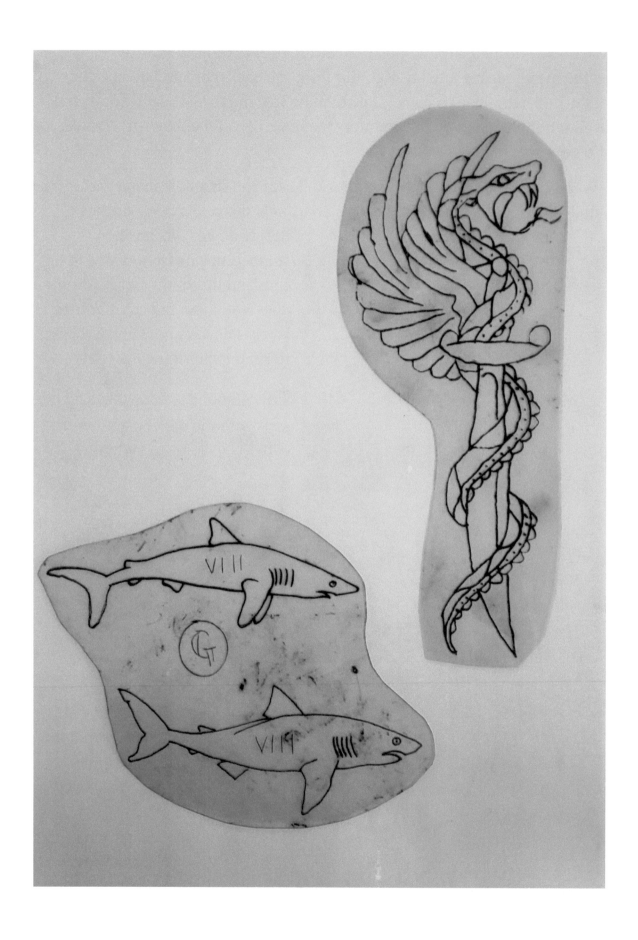

These were drawn in 1960 when I was four. Nice Dad included my name, BUT, look at the company I'm keeping!

The winged snake and 2 sharks were also on that flash sheet!

These days tattooers use individual little cups or caps to hold the pre-dispersed ink. Thin and runny is the best way to explain, like a stain, hard for us to get used to. Buddy made wooden blocks approx. ½" high 2 1/2" long and ¾" wide. He/we (including me and sis at early ages) would operate the drill press making a

 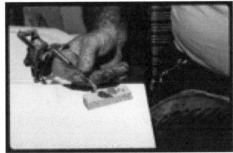

hole in each one for the black ink which was liquid. One for every customer. Carolyn & I as kids stood on a wooden box to reach the press. Next, he would put the

blocks in the dryer to spin off any loose sawdust. What a racket that made! (Remember we thought every kid grew up like this!) Wood absorbs liquid so he found a way to "French fry" the blocks. He filled an old Fry-o-lator with melted paraffin wax and placed the blocks in the basket just like he was making dinner. The blocks were now coated with a thin layer of wax. Into a large paper bag they went, still hot, for a few shakes to remove any extra wax. Perfection! We could also blend shades of color on the block like a pallet. To hold the blocks in place on the work counter Buddy hot glued a thumb tack face up and pushed the block over it. When he was a smoker he had thumb tacks glued to the front of his sign bench and next to his sink at the shop to hold the lit cigarette by the filter, ready for the next puff!

The wall of more up to date flash we added to the other side of the shop, an exterior wall, looked great. I hand colored all the designs to match how we intended to have them look when finished. My 1st try became a tie-dyed looking runny mess after a heavy rain. Just another challenge in an old building!

Excerpts of Buddy and Ronnie Daigle talking at Buddy's 80th Birthday party in the shop (2004):

"Aaah the old days... Remember using a sponge to wash the guys tattoo?... Remember dumping some more alcohol into the bucket holding the sponge?... It was the cleanest thing we had... Remember using a napkin for a bandage and no tape?... Remember trying to use a couple of elastics to hold it on... and they would tear it right off... Remember Sailor Rox would swish the tube out in the bucket and blow in it to get the water out? He used toilet paper and paper tape to patch a guy up. Remember the old red would blow up in the sun because of the mercury in it?...Remember the brown was made from rust oxide?... "

Ronnie was on Eddy Street in Providence, a very tough neighborhood. Metal bars on all windows greeted customers. In my reading of the articles Buddy collected I came across one from 1973 in the Brown Daily Herald interviewing Ronnie. I didn't know you could repeatedly use the word fuck that many times back then in a single article and have it printed! He said he has seen more guns in his shop than the National Guard had. He was quoted in the article, when asked what he thought of tattooing women more often now, he said, "I treat the broads just like I treat the guys." He also tattooed some of the bike clubs from MA and RI. Buddy and Ronnie both had asked the Clubs not to cause any shit in Newport or Providence because they would get thrown out of business. Eventually a member of a Club would get good at tattooing and we would see less of them. Of all the Club stencils I've come across while writing this I didn't see one for the Side Winders. Then I remembered! A member was telling Buddy about another member doing some tattoos. Buddy smiled and handed him the stencil to take with him.

NAPKINS:

There was another rig to hold 300 count white Scott napkins. He would slit the folded end with his straight razor about ½ deep. Pushing your index finger down on the top of the stack made it easier to grab about an inch of untorn napkins at a time. Then tear at the fold. Napkins torn at the fold, even without a slit, tear evenly. Half a

napkin worked perfect for wiping during the tattoo. An old timer Buddy had gone to visit was cutting napkins in half with scissors as he walked in. Buddy said, "Let me show you something." The old guy couldn't believe it! We've seen some artists

wipe constantly. Why irritate the skin more than need be. For some It was almost like busy work, as they were thinking what to do next. You can think without so much wiping.

VASCELINE:

Plain old-fashioned Vaseline, would be applied to the skin after washing and shaving. 1960's rule, it had to be in a collapsible tube, not an open jar. Double dipping in an open jar is an infection waiting to happen. Several years before I started Buddy bought a new grease gun and warmed the Vaseline in a percolating coffee pot and poured it slowly into the gun. He made a rig to hold the gun and the only thing showing, sticking out of the wall, was the tip and the handle. Early 1990's, Buddy didn't want to give up his grease gun but we were about to be inspected for the 1st time by the Health Department. (I had to agree with him that technically it was in a tube...) A few weeks into my job Dad had asked me to refill the grease gun. My instructions, "Put the gun in the vice, heat up the Vaseline in the coffee pot and pour it in." I did. He should have said **WARM,** not heat. As I poured it in it leaked out the bottom, all over the floor. What a mess!

The autoclave was on his left also tucked into the wall only sticking out a couple of inches. Far out enough to hold the 6 bullets of different sizes on display from a 22 to a 50 caliber. I remember asking what those bullets were there for. He told me when a customer asks "Do you have a bullet I can bite on?" He'd say, "What caliber?" HA HA He also told me the display kept people guessing if there was a gun in the shop. I figured sure there was. So, one night I asked him. He said, "NO WAY!" I was very surprised at that answer. Before I could say anything, he said, "I'd be afraid I'd use it." An honest answer from a man who spent 3 of his younger years fighting the Germans. He did have a machete that he called his Mexican toothpick, in view, by the side of the sink. If a joking guy would say "I don't like it take it off" he'd pull out the machete, hold it up and jokingly offer to remove it.

Dad never shared his stories of combat with me. In the early 1970's Buddy found out there were now yearly Army reunions. He went alone to the first one. Turns out most guys had brought their families. Starting the following year, the four of us went. At the end of the annual banquet a guy would volunteer to host the next year. Many were held in the South and Southwest. They convinced Buddy to host one, since most had never been to the Northeast. The Biltmore in Providence, RI, was the hotel Mom chose. She planned the day trips with large busses to Newport and Boston. They were surprised by our New England accents and got very quiet when we went over the bridges connecting parts of Narragansett Bay. OK, some gasped out loud and two let out a scream. This gave Dad an annual outlet to be with his Army buddies. It seemed like they kept most of their war stories to themselves. One Friday night as we were leaving the shop, prob. 1 a.m., his station wagon (needed for the large Newfoundland dogs and capable of carrying a full sheet of 4' by 8' plywood with the back door closed) wouldn't start. We were parallel parked on the narrow, one way section of Thames Street. This busy street is the start of the tourist blocks. The cobblestone roads weren't designed for cars but for horses and wagons back in the day. Buddy had gained some weight at this point in his life so he handed me the tire iron and told me to get under the car and "give the starter a rap tap". Well because we were parked against the sidewalk I had to lay in the road! SO, the banging on the starter didn't work. We went back in the shop and called a tow truck. They said they were very busy but would get there eventually. Back to wait in the car. I remember I was exhausted and had a slight headache. Dad suggested I put my head back and close my eyes. Nice.   Then he said "I'll take first watch." What? Something about the way he said it... My eyes opened wide but I remember sitting very still and quiet as he talked. He told me about being on guard duty in the war. Sometimes it was so cold your teeth would chatter and you tried to make them stop, but you couldn't. He explained you became fearful that the enemy was going to hear it. Then he told me there was a difference in smells from the German gun powder and the American gun powder. They learned to tell by sound if a gunshot was from a foreign gun. He said they would take guns off dead Germans to use to set up the enemy. He said they would go into the houses and look for the root cellars and sometimes would find wine stored in these cellars. He said units helped themselves to eating and drinking. Most were grateful for the treats and didn't make a big mess. He said other units would take a shit in the living room and use the curtains as toilet paper. I had never heard such stories. I remember feeling honored he was sharing these things with me that night. He was telling me these stories like he was back there. This continued until the tow truck pulled up after 3 a.m. The tow driver's door opened and 3 empty beer cans rolled out onto the street. "Buddy, it's you! I wish I knew it was you! I would have come sooner", said the driver. He gave us and the car a ride all the way home, over a half an hour away.

SIZING THE DESIGN: Be realistic! Leave a little room for the tattoo to spread over time. Guys would come in with intricate album covers and say they wanted it on their forearm! Buddy was still using the machine in the picture when I started, to vary the size of a picture. Plug in the frayed cord on the Bristograph and place a piece of glass over the picture to protect it from the heat. "Focus" it on the wall and trace the image as fast as you could on a piece of paper. I felt like I was chasing the image because the machine never stopped swaying slightly back and forth and there was a real chance if you took too long the picture was literally going to burst into flames. The focusing was done by moving the machine closer or further from the wall. The 2 walls making up my back room stopped about 2 feet from the ceiling. Buddy had nailed a 2x4 across the room and "made a rig" to hold that heavy old machine up by 2 metal straps. On top of the 2x4 was an old set of roller skate wheels for the machine to travel on. It did work pretty good! (Probably came from the same roller skating box he got from his brother.)

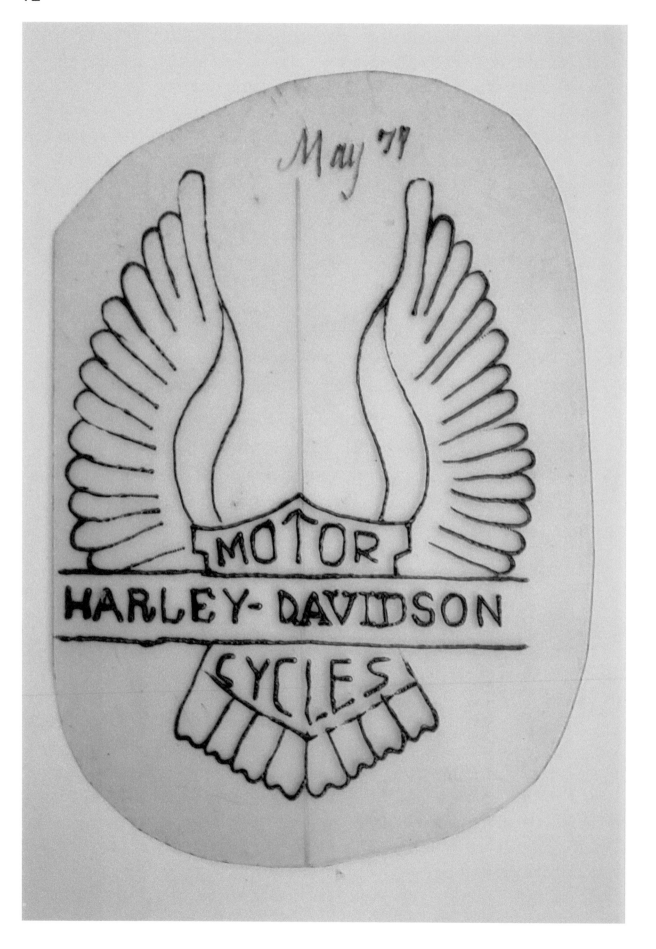

Buddy was a pioneer in re-purposing. (Somewhere between an ingenious thought and having to make do with what they had, or didn't have growing up.) Another transfer choice was drawing the design on the customer with a pen. (Ink poisoning might be a myth, we never had a problem.) After taking several minutes sketching the guy would say, "Can you make it a little bigger/smaller…" Start again!

 1984 National's Convention in Philly and Huck Spaulding was showing off the "Lucy". A lighted drawing table with 2 sets of handles and assorted controls for the focusing of the camera style shudders. WOW we couldn't place the order quick enough. Upon arrival Dad wanted to slightly modify it, putting the switches in one spot. He was happy that he had made the machine a little more efficient to use and asked me to try it out. Standing on the cement floor in the back room I hit the on switch. I was all but electrocuted! Turns out he was so taken by this great machine that he forgot to re-connect the ground.

Next, we still had to cut the acetate stencil with an engraver, just deep enough to hold some charcoal powder. Always starting the tattoo outline from the bottom working your way to the top trying not to smudge the faint design with your hand.

Tattoos as a general rule look best on the arm facing forward. Eagle designs look better with the head turned slightly. Instead of cutting 2 eagle stencils, one for each arm, he would put both heads on the stencil but had to remember to wipe away the charcoal of the other head!

Guys would ask what was in the old salt shaker he was sprinkling on the stencil. His answer more often than not, "Gun powder."

A TIP: DON'T CLOSE THE END OF A BANNER UNTIL THE LETTERING IS DONE.

We covered HARLEY DAVIDSO, done at another shop. There was no room for the "N" in the closed banner!

A few years later Sailor Ron invited us up to his shop to see his new copier complete with a mirror image feature and a "blue machine" (a machine that put blue dye on tracing paper where all black lines were on a design). It took about 4 seconds to make a transfer. I glared at Dad and said, "Why don't we have set of these machines!" Wet and set! NO more cutting stencils with that noisy engraver! The stencil paper was put on the skin using a variety of solutions. Speed Stick with Menon was the first one everybody was using, by rubbing the stick on a napkin and then on the skin. Baby shampoo diluted with water worked ok. We were told shops were using something else that worked fantastic! Health Dept. wanted things labeled at this point, SO, he broke out the black Sharpie Marker and wrote on the spray bottle S.T.S. short for Stencil Transfer Solution. Sounds good! Spray a bit on the skin and some customers had a look of – what's that familiar smell? Before they could say anything we made a statement with a smile, "Everybody says it smells like Pine Sol"...then changed the subject. (It was a little Pine Sol and a lot of water.) I'm sure there are professional products for sale these days.

"B" IS FOR BUDDY

We would get asked all the time "Is it true that there's a "B" in every tattoo?"

Over time guys would come in to get another tattoo and say proudly that they had found the B in the previous one. If a guy said he couldn't find it Buddy would tell them to "Keep looking." Urban legends get started that way, or do they?

Buddy's other standard answers:

Customer question: " How long have you been doing this? "
 Answer: "Two weeks tomorrow, not counting the Holiday. "

Interviewer's question: "What got you into this?"
Answer: "I didn't want to work for a living."

MORE TIPS: Protect the customers clothes. We always used a lap cloth or apron and a paper towel tucked and folded over their clothes. They may not thank you for keeping their clothes clean, but you'll know there mad if ink spatters and ruins theirs! Three things in life are certain: Death, taxes and tattoo ink doesn't come out of clothes. Also: state on your sign-in form that dyes and inks are used. Ask about known allergies. We also included the phrase "including human error" as to what we weren't liable for.

 Find a place to tuck your machines out of sight when you leave for the night. Obviously, we didn't have cameras, once it was gone, it was gone. Buddy always found a hiding place usually up and under the sink cabinet. He started hiding the machines out of sight after he was broken into in the early 70's. There **was** a window in the bathroom that the crook came in thru. They got the one machine on the counter and a little color and out the front door they went. This is what started the heavy bar across the entrance door. The door opened out. He said, "If they get in, I'm not going to make it easy for them to get out."

BEST TIP:

SHAVE IT TWICE **After washing and shaving the skin we applied the stencil transfer solution and put the blued paper stencil on. We let it dry for a ½ a minute or so then rubbed ointment into the skin. BUT then we shaved it again! It did remove some of the extra blue dye and re-shaving pushed the ointment into the pores. The excess ink on the black outline beaded along the line, no spatter. The wiping became more of a gentle dabbing than wiping. Fantastic! Try it!**

(A straight razor is all we had at the shop. Buddy didn't like the way hair clogged a safety razor. It took some courage to get used to using it!)

At the end of a tattoo after washing it, we had to give the new tattoo a quick spray of rubbing alcohol and it stung. Guys would ask, "What the hell was that!" Buddy didn't say rubbing alcohol … the answer depended on your new tattoo. If you had just gotten a panther, he'd say it was "Panther Piss". A rose, "Rose Water". A Ying Yang, "Ying Yang Piss"… snake piss…

The sailors if they were caught drinking way too much and on several occasions were given a medication. If while on the medication they drank alcohol or got any on their skin they would become violently ill. Sailors made sure to tell Buddy if they were taking the medication and he would take that spray bottle and hide it away so he wouldn't make the mistake out of force of habit, and use the rubbing alcohol on them.

"TAPING A GUY UP" AND AFTERCARE:

At the end of the tattoo we would put a couple of napkins over the new tattoo and tape them in place. Buddy got tired of fighting with the tape and "made a rig", a tape cutter. This slipped over your thumb, was made of an old can, had a serrated cutting edge and worked like a dream.

You feel like a broken record but it is important for customers to understand the aftercare instructions. The 70's was to the point. The printed instructions actually said: Before you crash take the bandage off, wash it with soap and water and keep your crummy fingernails off it and don't pick at the scabs. That does sound gross. (Gross, that 80's word again). To be more professional in the 80's keeping up with the times, we'd run thru the instructions for after care explaining: Wash your hands, remove the bandage in about an hour. Wash with mild soap and water daily using your hand, not a wash cloth and pat dry… If a guy was only half listening during the spiel Buddy would throw in at the end in a serious voice, "Remember NO drinking for 3 hours and NO sex for 90 days". **WHAT!** Buddy would wait a few seconds before he told them he was kidding.

A full moon story: The guy says after the run thru of aftercare instructions ,"SO, you want me to put gasoline on it and light it on fire?" Buddy responded, "Go right ahead"…

ANOTHER RIG:

It seemed in Newport in the 80's we lost power quite a bit. Usually for under an hour, at times much longer, but you never knew. We would light the flashlight and customers would still ask to sign in like business as usual and ask what time would be their turn… We heard Ron was just sitting up at his shop with a lit Bic lighter. We all should have gone home. One night a guy was signed up, his turn was next, getting the lettering "NO FEAR". The shop was crowded and power went out. Dad was excited about trying his newest rig. He had made a series of wires and a couple of small lights that could be attached to a car battery. He hands me the keys to his car and a wrench and says to a guy, "Skip, go help her get the battery out of my car." Could he have bought a spare friggin' battery! Back in business with the car battery sitting on the floor connected to the machine. You could have fried an egg on the lights. BUT of course, the rig worked and NO FEAR looked a bit fearful getting his tattoo.

MYSTERY RIGS: You tell me and we'll both know.

Guessing the one on the right could have an air gun tip soldered on. Maybe a quick way to attach a compressor and blow any excess water out of the tube after washing between colors… Eventually we were told we couldn't rinse the tube under our sink faucet. Hey, we drink that!

THE LOVE OF BIKES:

Buddy's first ride was a very used motorcycle. He was 16. It was the only ride he

could afford. When it rained, he got wet. I heard from his friends he got good at riding down the street in front of his house standing on the seat. In his later years Buddy often said he was surprised to still be alive."I didn't think I was going to see 21." (Between the Evil Knievel type stunts and fighting in the War.)

I think he made that fairing shown below. So wish I knew more about that. Buddy tells of his early days riding; One of his best lifelong friends he met when he was about 17. A guy named George Mayhew (pictured on the dedication page) from a couple of towns over, broke down right in front of Dad's family's house. Between the two,

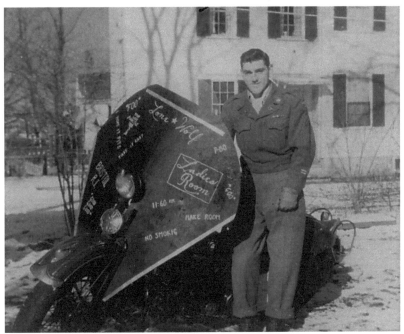

they got the bike going. The two guys, young and adventurous and with very little money, took a ride to the Catskill Mountains in Upstate NY. George was lead bike. Buddy sees George start to drive erratically and pulls over. While singing a song (constantly) a bee flew in George's mouth and stung him in the back of the throat. They found the 1st

drugstore and headed for the tweezers. Dad pulled the stinger out, wiped the tweezers off, put them back on the sale rack and off they went.

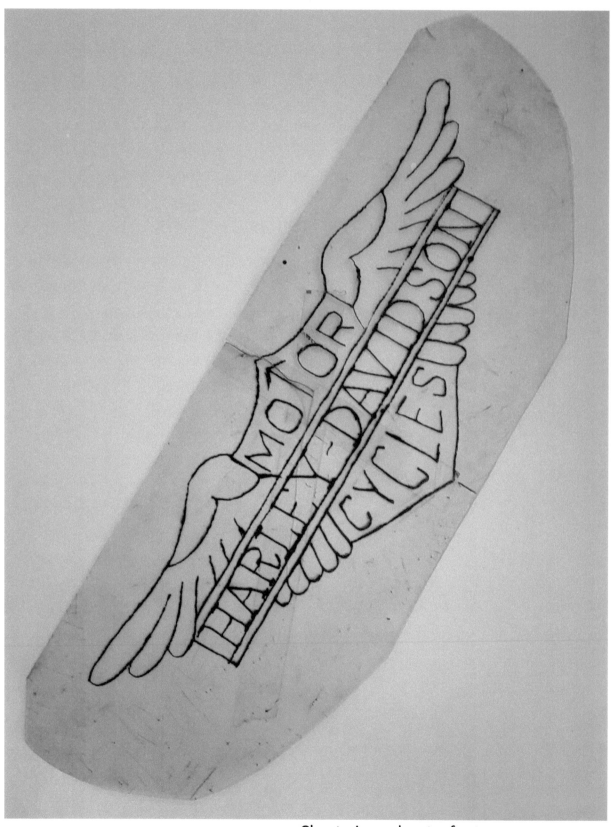

Chest piece about a foot across.

I remember he didn't have a bike when I was growing up. He said that was way too dangerous with all the people on the road...I was about to graduate from college and one night on his way to work he just pulled into the Yamaha dealership and bought a bike. Next, Joe got a bike too. Either the

roads had become less crowded (HA) or he figured he had done his job being responsible raising 2 daughters. Then Dad bought a Harley. The bike ran ok - not great. We would take the bike to work and park it **in** the shop so he could "keep an eye on it." Two bikes parked in the small shop! The whole shop was about 13' wide by 25 long. The waiting area/bike parking zone was elbow to handlebar crowded, measuring about 13 by 12. A few times as a joke a customer (or Joe) would put a small spot of oil on the floor under Dad's bike. Buddy freaked, and crawled around on hands and knees looking for the leak. Next, he bought a full dressed Honda. Should have measured the doorway of the shop, it didn't fit!

Two of the best dressed motorcycle riders I'd ever seen came into the shop carrying top of the line helmets. (I loved the old ad back when you had to start to wear a helmet: "If you've got a $10 head buy a $10 helmet.") One night a customer asked, "What's up with that?" He said he saw the 2 well dressed bikers that just left the shop get into a piece of shit car and drove off. They were wearing the whole 9; expensive leather jackets, chaps, boots...Dad said that happens from time to time. In the 70's he nicknamed a guy Counterfeit. Same thing, very well dressed, spending money on top-of-the-line riding clothes and then couldn't afford the bike!

BUDDY
JUNE 12, 82'
HONDA - DAVIDSON

Guys can talk for days about bikes (I liked when they referred to them as a scoot), and one wrench story was wilder than the next. Seems like when other bikers hear about a guy in a bike accident the 1st question is "How's the bike?"

We tattooed a guy named Dale many times. He was a talented bike mechanic from New Bedford, MA. Dale and his wife Sparkie owned and operated D&S Cycle. Great people. They get to talking one night and Dad brings up the Harley he also owns, but doesn't ride much, because he said he doesn't trust it. Buddy jokingly makes the statement, "We should put a smooth-running Honda motor in the Harley." Dale took the challenge and after several rounds of fabrication, especially widening the frame, the HONDA-DAVIDSON was born. That bike was quite a novelty piece. A few years later the bike was turned back into a true Harley with the help of CJ and Shaw's Engineering Motorcycle Service & Repair in Bristol, R I.

Buddy engraved some of the chrome on his bikes. About 90% of the chrome on his 72 Harley is engraved. He also engraved Larry Bonoff's bike. He was the owner of the old Warwick Musical Tent. They traded for concert tickets, (the only time Buddy went to see The Beach Boys).

A BOAT, A BIG NECK AND A GANG: Looking back as a young girl starting in the tattoo business, I had lots to learn! I was signing in my first sailor (there were still some left in Newport in 1980) and I said, "What boat are you on?" Buddy said, "It's a ship! It's not a boat. A boat fits on a ship but a ship doesn't fit on a boat." **GOT IT**

One of my next questions to Dad, "Why does this tattoo of a lady have such a big neck?" The tattoo is of a woman with her fingers placed at the base of her neck. The neck looked slightly wider than it should be. Dad motions that I should tilt my head and view it upside down. WELL WELL Now it looked like she was playing with herself...

We would tattoo members of several different motorcycle clubs. They were nice enough and respectful to Buddy. He asked that they not cause any trouble in Newport because he would be closed down if they did. When you entered the shop a large sign said, "No booze allowed in the shop." I guess it got out of hand in the late 70's when every couple of guys brought a case of beer to drink while they waited. The new rule was drink outside or even better in the parking lot across the street. As the night would wear on some of the gals along for the ride would get the USDA GRADE A stamp on her ass or Property of _____. They didn't care about the "Privacy for the Ladies" shade. After a few drinks they started getting rowdy with each other..." What are you lookin' at ..." Buddy told them to knock it off and they did!

One night the door opened and in came a half dozen guys from a motorcycle club. Minutes later door opened again and in came another 5 or 6, from a rival club! I glanced at Dad out of the corner of my eye and he was pasty white! Oh CRAP!

I said to the first guy as I'm signing him in, "What gang are you with?" Immediately I hear Buddy's voice say, "IT'S A CLUB!!!" Ooops, got it. "What would you like to get?" I asked. Guy looks me straight in the eye and said, "I want a fly tattooed on the head of my dick." Well, I don't have an answer for that. (I take some comfort in that we're in Newport, the old Navy regs are still in place...No hands, feet, face or private parts and at least to this point we have not.) Buddy chimes in, "No problem." I can't believe what I'm hearing! I know a city bus goes by the shop every hour. I'm picturing myself on the next bus never to come back. Buddy continues, "First I'm going to have to numb it, I'm going to hit it with a hammer." Everybody (but me) HA HA HA "Buddy how the hell are you..." All for my benefit...

84

A SPECIAL BOTTLE FOR FRATERNITIES:

The most popular URI Fraternity we worked on was Phi Gamma Delta. They (five to ten at a time) would get their Greek letters on the inside of their ankle. Boat shoes and no socks were trendy and some feet really stink. He gave the foot a quick squirt after they kicked off their shoe. It was cheap aftershave but it smelled better than ripe feet! Buddy told of a sailor paying $10 in ones using his sock for a wallet. The money had to be aired out overnight.

 Tattooing is a job where you take the good with the bad... part contortionist and a strong stomach for the variety of nasty body odors.

NO PERSONAL CHECKS:

The last check we took for a tattoo was written by a girl from a small town in Connecticut. I think it was $40. It bounced. Buddy was mad. It was returned to us stamped across the front "insufficient funds" Buddy displayed it on the wall next to a new sign "NO Personnel checks". One night several members of a bike CLUB came down and said they drove through that town on the way here. Buddy took the check off the wall and gave it to them. He said "if you want to collect it from her, have some beers on me"... I think about that once in a while as I'm writing a check.

TEACHING:

The tattoo business is opposite of AVON. They sold (sell - I think they are still in business) women cosmetics door to door and thru small parties. Every person you could convince to join the business and sell, you got a percentage of their sales! The company grew fast, selling to women everywhere. In contrast, there was only a limited amount of people wanting to get tattoos back then. Creating more tattoo artists potentially cut your own throat. If a guy would come to a shop with a tattoo machine for sale the shop owner would generally buy it just to get it off the street. Showing someone the trade was NOT done very often. I came across several hand written letters from people asking to be taught or asking to be shown a few things and answer a few questions. One guy from Canada wrote in September of 1980 that he was turned back at the border on his way to hopefully purchase an Electric Crayon. Another guy, a scrimshaw artist from the Virgin

Islands, said he had picked out a larger work space and wanted to offer tattooing too. He was hoping Buddy would call him collect and teach him a few things! My father in all his years did give quite a few pointers to those who asked. I remember three ladies called and asked if they could come in and watch us do a few tattoos. It was winter and we invited them down. They were hard to understand because they had heavy accents. They brought their pen shaped tattoo machine purchased thru the mail and showed us baggies of used needles with names on them for when they work on the same person again! They kept talking about a 3 day seminar coming up. We finally told them to pay attention during the class and all their questions should be answered then. Well we misunderstood! The lady that spoke the better English said, "No, we teacha the seminar, the permanent make-up." We didn't know what to say!

The 1st guy Buddy taught was in the early 60's. He was a family friend named

Chuck Marshall. Chuck was planning to tattoo in San Jose, California. He was quite successful. We visited his horse ranch in Morgan Hills. It was impressive overlooking the valley. Thirty plus years later Chuck talked to Buddy about moving back and tattooing

somewhere in Rhode Island. He starting palling around with my Mother and Father like the big brother I never had, riding shot gun in the front seat and Mom in the back! Buddy got involved helping Chuck find a shop to open in Woonsocket, the opposite corner of the state. Chuck is

pictured here on the right. They were in contact with a guy who was thinking of selling a shop because of health issues. They actually went to look at it a few times. We were at a tattoo convention in Montreal and a fellow RI artist asked Buddy if he had seen last week's local newspaper. A guy was applying to the Middletown Council for a tattoo license. He said the name, "Charles Marshall". (What a complete asshole!) Buddy couldn't believe it! Chuck's shop opened one town away, a couple of miles up the line on the main road, catching some of our flow of customers from Massachusetts. We had to drive by it on our way to work.

The other guy in the photo is Tony Souto. They became friends as kids. Tony was a great guy and everything you could ask for in a true friend. A greedy Chuck also hired a young guy to work with him. A handful of years later Chuck became sickly and sold the business to Jerry Schwartz, the young guy he had been working with. We became friendly with Jerry, wasn't his fault. I'm still friends with him. After a few more years Jerry moved to Vegas and owns Rock & Roll Tattoo.

The 2nd guy Buddy taught was one of his good friend's son-in-law Rusty Ash. Buddy not only enjoyed his company but treated him like a son. Rusty, the oldest

Buddy Rusty 3/28/84
Spruce St - Prov.

of five boys was a talented artist. All five were big guys, well built, and rode large motorcycles. He had plenty of canvas to practice on and opened his own shop Artistic Tattooing about an hour from us in Providence. The name Rusty came from his red hair. Buddy spent from 1967 to 1969 teaching Rusty, hanging out and having fun together.

He told me about the guys working at the toll booth they went thru nightly, would say they were really heading to Newport to meet up with some ladies. This went on night after night. One night on the way to work Buddy pulled over at the JC Penny store to do some shopping. Buddy bought a bottle of the cheapest perfume he could find and the largest pair of white ladies' underpants they had. On the way home he drenched the bloomers in the

perfume and tossed them into the toll booth as they sped off.

By the late 1970's Rusty claimed one in five getting tattooed was "a chick". The girls mostly got something small, but there was always a few that would surprise you with their requests. After the movie Jaws came out he found himself doing at least a shark a night. If customers would ask how long the tattoo would last, he would say, "About 6 weeks after you're dead, if you have a good undertaker."

In 1995 a local group of artists and photographers were planning a trip to Greece. Rusty's wife Linda asked Buddy to join them. My Mom said she didn't want Dad going alone and asked me to go with him. She volunteered to help with my young son. It was great, and, as we found out, it was Rusty's first trip abroad. Dad and I arrive at Logan Airport in Boston. We did know a few of the group and then were introduced to the rest. Next there is commotion in the airport. My suitcase is beeping! My mother had given me a travel smoke detector and put the batteries in it. Something pushed up against it... They flung my suitcase off in the corner, called security and made me go open it. It was not like the panic would be today but very embarrassing to say the least. Arriving in Athens and are exhausted, we still had another ride in a small plane to the Isle of Santorini and then a bus ride up the side of the volcano rim with no guardrails to the top known as OIA. It is believed that Santorini was known as the Lost Island of Atlantis. After the eruption of 1600 BC the center of the volcano collapsed leaving a crescent ring. The houses are crowded down the rim with the narrow road only at the top. We are checking in and instead of a room number you

just had to remember how many stairs down to your room. (Photo courtesy of Lou Cirillo). Thirty-seven was not the number Rusty wanted to hear. Dad and I were being shown to our room on the upper flat part and the guy asks me if I've had any Greek milk this morning (the licorice liquor Ouzo). NO – BUT HE DID!

Rusty was off to rent a car. He loved his classic cars and bikes as much as tattooing. He had in mind the largest, nicest and shiniest one they had. A short time later in a small, beat up, muffler-less piece of shit with crank windows is Rusty with a big smile on his face. He said the other cars were worse. This one had the "better" brakes! Many jokes were made about that. Every restaurant had a cat sleeping in a chair in the restaurant. There were no menus. Plates of sample food were displayed in cases, all you had to do was point. They NEVER looked anything like the sample, but were good. There was a steep cable car to get down to the ocean but we rode donkeys down the winding path and took the cable car back up. The scenery was absolutely beautiful. The white stucco buildings with blue domes, many bell towers and small sardines drying on clothes lines were common sights. We went home back thru crowded Athens and visited a local tattoo shop. The long plane ride home was spent looking at a bride alone, in full wedding dress, veil and red lipstick. She looked a little rough by the end of the trip and I don't recall seeing a groom waiting in Boston... Our group was separated on the plane. We sent, "Are we there yet?" messages in an empty wine bottle to Rusty passing up towards the front of the plane row by row and many passengers signed it too. At some point we're all exhausted and I hear Rusty say to Linda, "watch close when they stamp my passport cause you're not going to see that happen again." We all took beautiful pictures and had a great time. Rusty eventually taught his brother Dean. He also taught his sons Dean and Greg the art of tattooing. Rusty passed away September 2021. Heaven must be getting pretty crowded.

The 3rd guy was a character from a well to do family that owned a race track.

He wanted to be a tattoo artist. He was well educated, sailed and dove all over the world chasing treasure. He repeatedly came and hung around in the shop wanting Buddy to teach him. Buddy wasn't interested. It is lots of work to properly teach someone the trade. Ron Dario started getting a few tattoos and hid them all from his family. Buddy did a tiger and a dragon on the cheeks of his ass. Early 1970's, one night Ron said Ruby (from up the street) had agreed to teach him. Only then did Dad agree. Ron Darth was his 1st aka. (Star Wars movies were very popular) Ron then got a big leather bag, like a mailman bag, to carry his tattoo equipment around in and travel with. The next aka: Ron Darth Postman. Next line on the card: Always Rings Twice". "Sailor" Ron opened his own shop the Gold Doubloon in Providence. We asked Ron to take over the 3rd and final shop license available in Newport before someone else could. Hobo was moving to New Hampshire. Ron was hardly ever open because he was travelling or making X- rated movies. I remember the three of us going for a pizza and he pulls out a pack of pictures from his latest trip. It was a nude cruise! I'm trying to eat a pizza at a table with my father, looking at Ron do a back float in the pool on the ship naked. I pointed out he had pants on in another picture. I learned that when you went skeet shooting off the deck or having dinner in the cruise ship's restaurants you had to wear pants. TMI.

 Chance Wilder was his movie name. I learned when he got back from the Vegas Adult Movie Awards there were specific categories. A movie with S & M could not also have traditional sex. The young guy I was working on looked quite surprised when Ron was telling me about the movie winning an award in the "All Anal" category! The things you can learn. (I should have known. The name of the movie was Dr. Butts.) Ron and our family became friends. We didn't want anything from him, the friendship and stories were enough. Many had tried to take advantage of the handsome guy with some money. During the first year of Buddy teaching Ron, they went to a Tattoo Convention is Amsterdam. Every time over the years when that would come up, Dad couldn't get the smile off his face. After the convention we met up with them on a ski trip in Switzerland. My mother rented an apartment for a week, (I was in high school) our family, one of my sister's friends and Ron. Dad said he was a little nervous, "Like putting a fox in a hen house." The first afternoon Ron suggested we take a walk to the Club Med. I don't know how he got us in - we weren't staying there... Somebody handed him a few beads to get us a couple of drinks with. We then watched a game. Reminded me of musical chairs but there were no chairs. The men laid face down in a circle, heads towards the center. The women paraded around the men and when the music stopped the gals jumped onto a guy's ass with their high heels on! There was also glittered face painting. The designs were so beautiful and intricate, we got 1 each. When

RON BY
ED HARDY
JUNE 17 82

we got back to the apartment Dad just shook his head. Ron took off the next day with a free-spirited chick he had met at the club. They wandered throughout Europe in her VW Bug. He did come home weeks later. Ron's Mother in the meantime was calling my Dad asking when was the last time anyone saw him.

Ron got friendly with Ed Hardy in California. Ed studied in Japan and was starting to do tribal style tattoos. He covered most of the tattoos on Ron's ass and legs with the newly popular black, thick, tribal designs. He came back and showed us.

Very impressive to see a guy so covered. Dad being a wise guy asked Ron what tribe he was with. Ron loved to show off his legs and dropped his pants at both of my wedding receptions for all the guests to see. Ron told interviewers over the years he was taught by Buddy Mott and paid him for doing so in gold doubloons. NOT TRUE! Dad was so mad. He was all shook-up thinking someone was going to try and break into his house to steal the gold doubloons HE DIDN'T HAVE! Security systems were not a thing yet. We did have "Wentworth Alarm Co." stickers on the windows of our cars. There was no such company and no doubt they were made on his printing press. Oh, and a sign posted in the garage window "Never mind the dog, beware of the owner" written under a picture of a gun barrel facing you. Ron sadly passed in 2016. I miss him. He brought the Club Med photo of us with the painted faces from the 70's to my Dad's wake to make us smile.

MY FIRST TATTOOING EXPERIENCE, 1980:

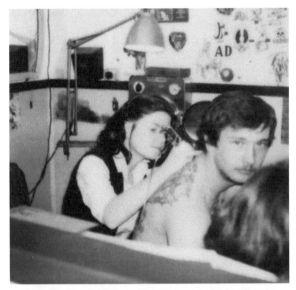

There were 2 guys that came in quite a lot. Buddy had mentioned to them he was going to teach his daughter. They both had back pieces started. Buddy told them he was looking for a couple of canvasses for me to work on. This guy, let's call him Vinny, already had Dad's large sailing ship tattooed on his chest. I heard years later the deal was "if I screwed it up he would fix it!"

(No gloves).

Billy Mac had the second back piece started by Buddy that I worked on. This photo is the work in progress. It is a fantasy piece with a Viking ship coming over the mountains.

92

Right time, right place. Bill was in the shop the night a photographer came in and took lots of pictures. They can be seen on the Library of Congress website under Photos, Prints and Drawings then search Buddy's Tattoo Newport RI or Buddy Mott. The photos were taken in September 1979 by Henry Hornstein for the Rhode Island Folklife Project. Collection AFC 1991/022, American Folklife Center, Library of Congress.

More photos from that night can be seen on the website listed above.

Bill also was in the shop one night, pre-1980, when a VIP invitation arrived to an event in NYC. Buddy was happy with the invitation but said he didn't plan on going even though it was during the week and not on a weekend. (Eventually, Buddy started taking Wednesday nights off. We should apologize to some of our friends and relatives for leaving wedding receptions after the soup, cause it was a Saturday and we were going to work. In 1978 the Catholic Church finalized my Dad's annulment from his brief wedding in the 1940's. Mom and Dad, married in 1953 in a Civil Ceremony, were finally able to take their vows in a Catholic Church. It was ON A WEDNESDAY, his day off. I was 20 years old. At the dinner after the waitress was confused when we started dinging the glasses so the 'Newlyweds' would kiss. She asked what the occasion was and I told her, "My parents just got married".) Back to the invitation on the next page. Bill went and said it was wild!

Annie Sprinkle and Spider Webb

cordially invite you to a gala

TATTOO PARTY

at the

HELLFIRE CLUB

in celebration of Charles Gatewood's

new book

FORBIDDEN PHOTOGRAPHS

published by R. Mutt Fine Art Editions

Time: Wednesday, Oct. 14, 9pm 'til dawn

Place: Hellfire Club, 28 Ninth Ave, N.Y.C. (13th st.)

Dress: Tattoo and Sexy

Admission: ~~Ten Dollars~~ *YIP + 2*
NO CHARGE
Cg

Party with:

Spider, Annie, Charles, Kenneth Anger, Mam'selle Victoire,

Mick Jagger, Fakir Musafar, Original Sin, Maud Adams,

Bruce Dern, The Former Marco Vassi, Mark Jury, Kandy Kane,

The Electric Crutch Band, Mark Stevens, special surprise guests,

and of course hundreds of heavily tattooed people.

BRING YOUR CAMERA!

A NEW SIGN:

This sign that Buddy routed hung next to the entry door for as long as I can remember. He made a special screwdriver, ground to just 2 prongs to fit in the top of the carriage bolts. That was supposed to make it harder to rip it off the building and happy to say it remained in place.

1991 What a nice surprise! Dad without a word had gone to Newport earlier that day to hang the new sign that included my name! He made the lettering using his band saw.

Here are some more examples of his woodworking. He liked to make a project on a single piece of wood, the longest being "The United States of America."

Then he challenged himself some more and made a 3 foot Titanic that lit up. His 2 Grandsons were young at the time and casually asked if they could each have one. Grandpa made a total of 3.

It's **1995 my sister Carolyn** joined us and turn the tables...

I became the practice canvas!!

She enhanced my heart tattoo made up of a variety of small flowers. There are also a few flower pieces that have broken off and are drifting away. A dove of peace carrying fresh flowers and ribbon flying towards the heart is part of the design too. My way of symbolizing the journey of life, adapting to the changes, seeking peace.

Stanley's Boatyard was near our house growing up. Dad would on occasion, in the afternoon, hand letter the names on the boats/yachts and make signs for the marina. Many times my sister and I got invited along. His nickname around the boat yard was Rembrandt.

My little/only and talented sister Carolyn still (since the 80's) hand letters and applies vinyl to transoms, life rings etc. I've gone to help a few times over the years. We've been balancing 15-ish feet in the air on a plank many times like trapeze artists. One sailboat was so big and the owners wanted a hand done gold leaf cove stripe on their 70 foot boat (2 sides)...She picked me up on Wednesday and dropped me off on Friday! Her son Leander helps her now (I'm smiling). Carolyn also joined us tattooing in the mid-90's. She worked with us for almost 10 years. It was great getting to spend that amount of time with her, watching as she experienced some of the things that we had gotten used to as normal. There was no internet etc. If we found a picture we liked we would tear it out of a magazine (while no one was watching) and these pictures grew to 3 large files of almost everything you could think of. Some customers would bring in a picture of an idea they had in mind. That was helpful, we were not total mind readers. I remember trying to steer people away from Smurfs and Aladdin. Way too much blue in the tattoo to see detail from a distance. One question a tattooed person should not have to answer is, "What is that supposed to be?"

Approx. 4 years into my job Dad decided I should take over Joe and Dave's jobs! I began signing in all customers, answering questions, answering the phone, assisting with customers out in the front who had or were about to pass out and finish coloring almost all of the tattoos, cleaning up at the end of the night and that included the empty beer cans in the bank's parking lot across the street. It was nice to have Sis there to help us out. Advice to make life easier: Listen to the customer as you walk them thru the process. Hire people with a sense of peripheral vision, capable of being aware of what is going on all thru the shop. Make one person responsible to "pre-flight" the opening check lists.

We (Buddy, my sister Carolyn and myself) also attended a few Tattoo Conventions together over the years.

Ron in the mid 1980's hosted, filmed and directed a mini- convention in Northern RI. He asked me to be on the panel of judges. I was also a judge at the Worchester, MA Convention in 2007.

Great fun!

Wayne and Pat Holmes from Color Creations in East Providence, RI, would come to the shop for a visit and show us where they were headed to the next Convention. They subscribed to all the tattoo magazines (pre-internet). One convention was at a large beautiful hotel that had booked two conventions on the same weekend, not unheard of. The two were the Tattoo Convention and a Baptist Convention!

One morning Lyle Tuttle called. He was in Providence and invited us out for breakfast. I turned around only for a second, he and Buddy were acting like convicts behind the gate of the restaurant.

This is one of my favorite pictures taken at a convention in Montreal. We have no idea who this guy is or where he appeared from and the lights line up great behind my sister's head making her look like a Princess. I had that picture taped behind my work area for years. I'd tell anyone who asked, that was my sister and her husband.

98

VACATIONS:

Growing up, the only way Mom could keep Dad from creating cool stuff all day in his cellar at home or going to Newport to tattoo was to get him out of town. They

included me and my sister on some of these wonderful trips to faraway places. Buddy completed his bucket list which included seeing the Northern Lights from Iceland, a camera Safari in Africa, skiing the Swiss

Alps and diving off a square rigger into the South Pacific Ocean. Seemed like wherever we went either in the USA or some faraway place, someone would say "Hey, Buddy!" Two that stand out: One in a gondola high in the air, on a ski trip in Austria and the other in an elevator in Fiji. These trips were partially paid for by Buddy's versions of various cartoons. My sister and I can also thank the characters and the characters who got them for helping to put us thru Providence College.

ANOTHER MEANING OF THE WORD "VACATION" :

 Conversation one night in the shop, Buddy said to a guy, "Where you been?" His response, "on vacation." They laughed. Next question, "How long were you away for?" The answer, "3 years." I said to myself that's one hell of a vacation. **JAIL** is where he was. He showed us a pretty nice tattoo done in the joint. He said they made the ink from burning pages from the Bible. Buddy offered the advice he heard that burnt toilet paper works better. His answer, "I'll remember that for next time!"

A group came in one night – for an opening line, a real ice breaker (with a heavy southern accent) "I got this in the Penitentiary." Got my attention…

Girl: "I want a Cesta." She doesn't look like a Jai Alai player. The guy says, "she's a pilot." OK, she wants a Cessna plane tattooed on her arm. I start signing her in and ask for a license. I'm waiting for her to whip out the pilot's license and wave it around. Who could blame her. "No – I have an ID. – NO, all I've got is my release papers from the Women's House of Corrections yesterday." !!! WOW! Over the years my son says I say WOW a lot. This is one of the examples of why…

Some guy named Jimmy comes in – says he's a friend of a friend and shows me an average sized tattoo he got years and years ago. He is back from 'vacation'. He said, "I got 15 years after I got this. I wonder what I'll get now – I want a dragon from my neck to my ankle." Another guy in the shop said softly what I was thinking: "He'll probably get the chair."

WORKING FOR THE FAMILY BUSINESS: (SO CALLED MATERNITY LEAVE)

In 1990 I was going to have a baby. I was due April 27th. As I got bigger and bigger people would ask "When are you due?" The closer we got to April 27th the more Dad thought I was going to explode, I guess. Well time went on, "When are you due?" asked repeatedly by nice customers. April 27, it was now May 4th. Dad said he wanted me to stay home starting the next day May 5. My son was born May 6. Thirteen days later Dad said, "It's getting really busy at the shop, I'll send your Mother to help your husband with the baby and you can come help me." WHAT?! Well working on a guy that first night back, the guy asked if I had any kids...how old...When I said 13 days he looked scared. I should have been. I did get some thoughtful handmade gifts. One gift I was told would bring the baby luck if I hung it over the crib... 5 chicken wishbones, polyurethaned and strung together with pretty ribbon. So, without much sleep you just keep going.

Never dreamed that my wonderful son (fake tats) would look like the cartoon drawing on the cover, partially shown below, of The New Yorker by artist A. Spiegelman. Google the full cover May 10, 1993. Picture my reaction the first time I saw this!

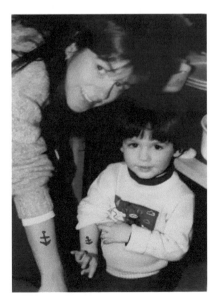

HANGING OUT WITH GRANDPA:

My sister and I have 1 son each, eleven weeks apart and none of that was planned. Grandpa loved drawing on Leander and Zack. The kids wanted big tattoo drawings. When he was done with them, it was their turn to draw on him.

The kids would get invited for a sleepover. Later when I would see the pictures I couldn't believe some of the projects he had them help him with. Replacing the flagpole with a ships mast was a big project. They were only 5! Buddy lived on the Palmer River. His flagpole was very visible as you crossed the bridge from Warren into Barrington. Yearly he designed and made Christmas light decorations that he, his friends and our families would help make and hoist up the flag pole. We weren't allowed to tell anybody what he was

going to make. Every year the decorations seemed to be getting larger and more elaborate. The decorated old wooden flagpole snapped one stormy December night. Probably a good thing, because, after it broke Dad was telling me how he was making a small bosun's chair so the kids could practice getting raised and lowered and eventually paint the pole! They were 3! **NO!!!**

The new pole was a large aluminum ship's mast that had broken off a sailboat. Buddy only wanted the part above the break and the price was right, free. (Compare the height with the guys standing below.) He put spot lights on the yardarms and a gaff-rig for the American flag. Guess who got to climb the ladder and replace the bulbs, (thankfully not the kids) me, the

small, short daughter!

Grandpa taught his Grandsons how to play pool as soon as they could see over the pool table. He also

made sure they knew how to swim and be safe around the water. The 16 foot jetboat he had with a 350 cu. in.

car engine (that no insurance co. would insure) came with the lettering inscribed on the back of the boat: *Get it, Sit down, Shut Up and Hang on!* The river in front of the house was shallow and the boat didn't draw much water. He bought the jet drive because there wasn't a prop, making it safer for waterskiing.

Buddy loved to feed all birds. The ones on the river would swim right over when

they heard the latch on the back door unlock. He didn't like the squirrels tearing up his bird feeder in the tree so, he made a rig that surprised even himself. He would hide in the garage and plug in the cord when he one on top of the feeder. The squirrel was supposed to get a little zap. The 1st time he tried it the squirrel's

legs went straight out and it fell to the ground smoking.

The next morning after one of these sleepovers, Zack with OJ in hand, positioned to clink the glasses together, said, "Aren't you going to say *cheers* Mommy?"

Looking back, I mostly worked with men and on men. The gay folks were refreshing and fun. We discussed fashion and color and the pretty curtains I made for my back room… Then in 1982 on a busy Friday night the TV show called 20/20 was on in the background. I'll never forget saying to Dad, "Listen to this, AIDS. Hope this doesn't become a household word." We were following all the rules of the day back then, no gloves or eye protection. We also cleaned with no gloves, just a paper towel and some kind of spray. I became uneasy tattooing my overly feminine friends that I spent quite a bit of time with. They were afraid too. We were learning more about the transmission, no cure or vaccine and a new phrase to us: bloodborne pathogens. When my son was 4 in the early 90's I was married and was told I had an infection in my mouth called Thrush, not a big deal, BUT, because of what I did for a living my doctor sent me for a HIV test. It took a full 2 long weeks for the results. I called Dad and told him I quit. I rarely/never swore in front my parents. He knew I was very anxious about my test and the waiting was killing me. He asked why I was quitting. Well, he asked and I told him, "If I have Aids it better be because I fucked the 5th fleet and not because I went to work on a Monday night." Of course, this was springtime and the season was right around the corner, so a few weeks later after the negative test result and much pressure from family I went back, with latex gloves on and glasses for eye protection!

OLD BUSINESS CARDS:

Buddy would make it a point to stop in and meet other tattooers where ever he went over the years and trade business cards. Both of the Newport shops had the same phrase on the cards. I think Dad came up with it first…doesn't matter: "For the very best in tattooing." He'd write back and forth with Terry Wrigley from Scotland and Cindy Ray, the famous heavily tattooed woman known as, "The Lady with the Classy Chassie." Carol Nightingale's card from Washington, DC referred to himself as, "The Man with the Golden Needles and Sophisticated Dermagraphics". A guy named 'Tom' Expert Tattooing, no phone or address, just, Best Work on the Coast. (What Coast?) The back had a cartoon monkey head and the words, "If you've been stung once, see us – we'll sting you better!" There was the Old Salt's Studio in San Diego, CA: "Where World Dignitaries & Celebrities Meet". Local bumper stickers ranged from Sin on Skin in Tiverton, RI: "SEE YOU IN HELL" to "I DID YOUR DAUGHTER LAST NIGHT BLOODY & ALL." Inflicting Ink in Portsmouth had, "GIVE BLOOD, GET A TATTOO". I also liked KJ's Modern Primitives in Providence: "FAITHFULLY TATTOOING ALIEN LIFEFORM SINCE 1988."

Not uncommon to have tattoo artists give themselves a title before their name like Captain, Sailor, Doc and Professor!

MEANINGS:

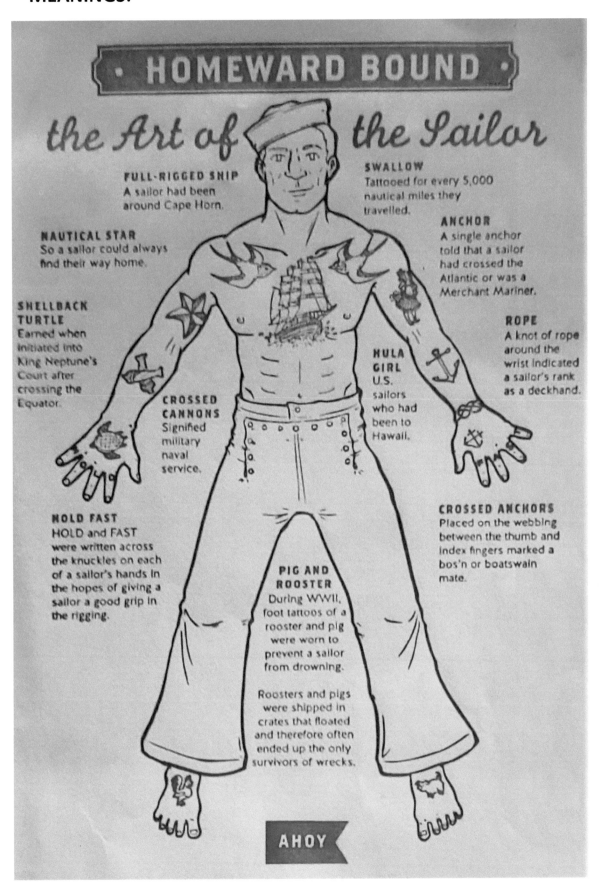

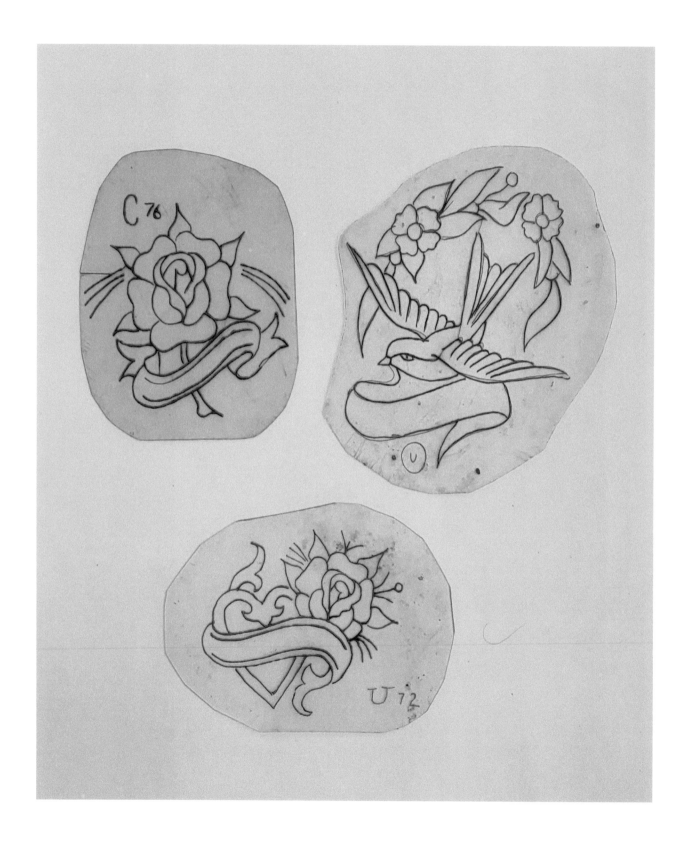

I'm signing in a guy one night and then ask his friend what he wants. He said, "someday to be buried in a Jewish Cemetery." I didn't realize until then it was a thing that if you were tattooed you couldn't be buried in a Jewish Cemetery. Leviticus 19:28 "You shall not etch a tattoo on yourselves." We would get a postcard once in a while in the mail, sent anonymously, stating that and telling us if we didn't stop tattooing we were going to hell...

DAD'S HAVE:

My Dad had my Mother's name, Madonna, tattooed on his upper arm and then my name Marilyn (the oldest) followed my sister Carolyn's name. As a kid I thought this

was standard. Have a wife and kids and the names, of course, were on the arm. He would also entertain us at friend's pools or at the beach by making the sailing ship on his chest float and then sink. The Hawaiian gal tattooed on his leg would dance when he flexed his muscles. Normal for a kid, right? I remember the first time I noticed a friend's dad with no tattoos. I felt like she was being gypped.

Thinking back Dad once said he wished he put the birthdates for me and my sister under our names. The older I got the more I was glad he didn't.

I remember walking into a friend's basement and seeing it empty, cement walls and the boiler. I thought every cellar had a sign bench, wood working machines of every kind, 2 lathes, printing press, welding equipment and tanks (he didn't mention the

tanks on the home owners insurance policy), a dart board and a pool table. One of my friends commented on his first trip to Buddy's basement, "Walt Disney would be jealous." Before the pool table, during the 1960's Buddy was building a Fallout Shelter in the corner the cellar. He had sent away for a full set of plans. That was during the Cuban Missile Crisis. He had most of the cinder block walls up when he realized he didn't quite have the height needed to stand. Some effort was made to dig up part of the cellar floor as the world was returning back to "normal". I remember playing in the

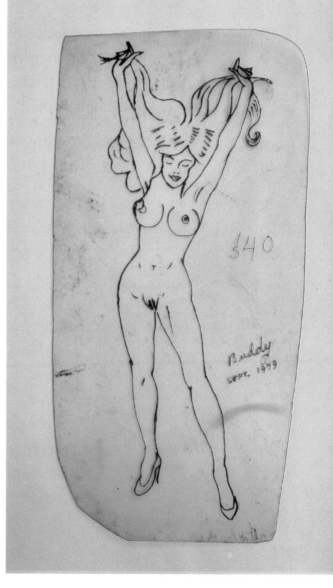

unfinished shelter for years with the neighborhood kids. Now it's 1974 and Buddy wants a pool table. I asked him as we're removing the cinder blocks, "What about the bomb shelter?" He said, "We'll hide under the pool table."

LISTENING:

A couple comes in and the guy wants to get her name. $40 bucks, 3 colors with a small star or heart and scroll work under it. Then you pick up on the conversation between the couple. "How do you spell your name?" They probably haven't been together long... "Don't get my name" and "You're wife is going to kill you" are 2 more comments that just got the guy a slightly larger name tattooed and for no additional charge! Buddy would say, "Like money in the bank." Nine times out of ten the guy would be back to have it covered by another tattoo and go figure, the small eagle or panther wasn't quite going to fit over it. Pull out the stencil for the larger more expensive one.

More money in the bank: Sailors would often get a sexy bare breasted girl tattooed, most with a sailor hat and panties. Over the next several years as the sailor had returned to civilian life and had a family, adding a bathing suit easily made the tattoo G rated.

"Only get your kid's name, can't go wrong with your kid's name..." Not true. A guy wanted his kid's name covered. We overheard, "I found out it's not my kid." I felt bad for Sammy Jr. who was about 12 years old.

PHRASES WE TATTOOED:

"YOUR NAME" tattooed on the ass. Guys would make bets, "I've got your name tattooed on my ass." Drop the drawers and there it is: "YOUR NAME" !!!

(Another popular tattoo was a rooster hanging by a noose tattooed below the knee. They would bet others that, "I've got a cock that hangs below my knee." Pull the pant leg up and reveal the hanging rooster...)

"The prettiest woman I ever kissed was another man's wife: My Mother".

Guy gets a large dragon and rose on his shoulder and the saying below: "No amnesty from the invisible prison." (?)

"This sailor will go to heaven because he did his hitch in hell."

DILLIGAF (Do I Look Like I Give A Fuck)

"Because You Deserve What Every Individual Should Enjoy Regularly." This was written out as a tattoo. He told us it stands for BUDWEISER.

ILMOTGF Ok, I was curious, I said I know this was none of my business... He could not believe I didn't know what that stood for! (In Loving Memory Of The Gambrinus Family), the makers of Corona beer. His mother must be so proud.

KISS (Keep It Simple Stupid.)

YCJCYAPOA with the male and female symbols. (Your Curiosity Just Cost You A Piece Of Ass.)

TRENDS:

"Come over here, hold this pencil for me." A phrase I quickly learned I didn't want to hear. That meant a guy was having a tattoo done on the inside of his lower lip. Yes, they drooled, it bled and they got black on their teeth...GROSS. We found if you wrapped the lower lip around a pencil it would help stretch the skin so the outline would take. All that for their name, nick name or the ever popular "Fuck You." (Buddy generally would not tattoo that phrase on a visible part of the body). How the world has changed.

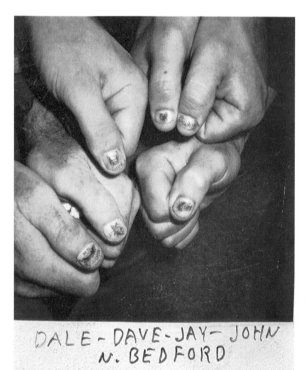

DALE - DAVE - JAY - JOHN
N. BEDFORD
10-25-82

Tattooing small designs on fingernails (mostly thumb nails) became popular for a while in the 80's. Using a single needle and pressing just enough to scratch into the nail a simple design, like a butterfly, looked nice. The night in the picture (Buddy tattooing on his 58th birthday and loving every minute of it) friends, mostly bike mechanics, came in to say "Hi." The designs got more and more elaborate that night, one wanting to outdo the other. HD, a winged wheel...all the size of scrimshaw. The nail took and held the color well. The nail grows out over a few weeks. This was before there were fancy nail shops on every corner doing intricate designs.

Crop tops for men with our logo! Light gray seemed to be the color of choice. Takes the eyes a second to focus and realize you are looking at a big,   non-tan, exposed (on purpose) gut! Thankful that trend was over quick.

Popular white T-shirts soon turned into everyone wanting black shirts. Buddy drew this design for his 40th Anniversary shirts. Designing for a black background can present some challenges. We bought a pin making gadget and Buddy set this type on his press too. (An extra challenge for a circle.) We passed out pins that also read: Official Member US Drinking Team (during the Olympic years), and

Toro Poo-Poo

(bullshit)

My most embarrassing moment at the shop:

Concentrating on a design I was coloring one night on a guy's chest using the rotary machine, my bangs got a little too close to the spinning cam shaft. I had to walk out to the front with the machine hanging from my hair, twisted right to the scalp! Buddy looked surprised and then 'gently' freed the cam with scissors! Didn't do that again!

TATTOO ID'S FOR DOGS:

This was a trend he gave up on pretty quick. Previously prize dogs were tattooed on the inside of the ear for an identifying mark. To prove a kidnapper had your dog, they'd cut off the ear and sent it to the owner. Well that permanently disfigured the dog. The next spot chosen became the inside of the leg near the belly. Buddy only made a couple of special trips to the shop to meet up with guys and their prize pit bulls. The muzzled dogs were scared and some pissed on the floor. I was surprised by the amount of owners that would openly brag, in disgusting detail, about how you introduce the pups to the scent of blood and how they fought their dogs. These owners started getting tattoos of the head of a pit all bloodied up with the name of the dog under it. One night an obnoxious dog owner was giving me a hard time and I said to Dad, "ENOUGH ALREADY!" not wanting to do anymore of that. The guy asked if he could just get some lettering instead. I was busy in the back and after got to see the guy's new tattoo:
"IF IT AIN'T PIT IT AIN'T SHIT."   That was the last one he did.

POPULAR TATTOO TRENDS OF THE DECADES:

1960's   A little red devil.
A skunk with Stinky written below it.
Sailor girls (some wearing more clothes than others).

"Man's Ruin" pretty much covers it.

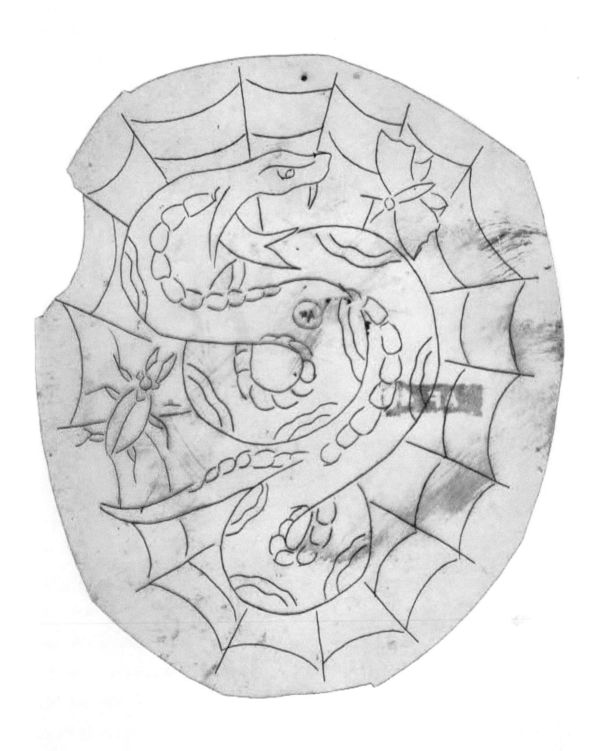

1970's Skulls, skulls wearing a variety of hats. (Pirate, cowboy, sailor, drive on rag, baseball... Grim reapers with the traditional scythe or holding a variety of other objects like skis, a martini glass...

Spider webs and black widow spiders on elbows mostly, knees too. (A few on the top of the head!)

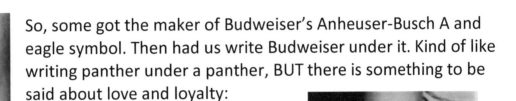

Harley Davidson #1 Logos, (only 1 Honda tattoo).

So, some got the maker of Budweiser's Anheuser-Busch A and eagle symbol. Then had us write Budweiser under it. Kind of like writing panther under a panther, BUT there is something to be said about love and loyalty:

It says, "MY FIRST TRUE LOVE"
Customers started getting creative with cartoons holding different stuff like a mug of beer, or a wrench (for the mechanic), giving the finger (pegging the finger...chucking the bird...) Buddy sketched the 1st raised middle finger with the cartoon's hand facing out, showing the thumb folded over the other fingers. It's the back of the hand that needs to face out. The one and only time I was demonstrating the 'proper way', new customers had just walked in as I was "flipping off" my father.

Sam, gun in one hand and beer mug in the other... A few years ago in Providence, at Ronnie's old shop, I had the pleasure of meeting Mark Mahoney from The Social Club Tattoo - Hollywood, California. I was surprised when he was telling Sam stories. He said if he was ever to do another one the guns would be pointing at the temples.

Pegasus, unicorns and wizards became very popular the 1980's. Usually we would add a rainbow in the background. Now the rainbow is the symbol for the gay community. The symbol of choice several decades ago, used to be a small pink triangle tattooed in an inconspicuous spot, usually the chest or ankle.

Realistic looking tigers and other animals became wildly popular thanks to the flash of Pinky Yun, Greg Irons and JD Crowe in the **1990's**.

If girls would come in and seem undecided as to what to get, we'd suggest, "Why don't you get matching tattoos, it's the 90's thing to do." One night my sister Carolyn got a beautiful waterlily tattoo. A couple of weeks later she had a small butterfly added above it to accent the flower. Out of nowhere she said to me, "Why don't we get matching tattoos, it's a 90's thing." So - we do have matching tattoos. We asked Dad at the end of the night what he was going to say to Mom when he got home about tattooing both of her daughters that night. His answer was simple and to the point. He said, "I'm not going to tell her." Could this be an example of why they were married for 61 years?

Then came tribal. Some pieces were very large and elaborate. It would take Buddy only 10 minutes to outline and me an hour or more to fill it in. The human body was enhanced with the tribal type designs also placed on the lower back. This elongated and beautifully accented the female figure. Someone eventually coined the phrase: "TRAMP STAMP". What a shame.....and that trend was pretty much over. I still think that area looks good tattooed.

Kanji is the name for symbols of an idea such as an object, thing or quality used in Japanese writing since the 5th century. Chinese script forms a major part of the Japanese writing system. These Oriental characters became very popular. The 1st one we did was on a guy who came in and said he wanted the one meaning FRIENDS. Dad said, "Do you have a picture?" He was one of many sent up to the Chinese Restaurant to have them to write it down. The guy came back with some characters written on a piece of paper. There are about 200 Chinese dialects! That night he either got the word friends or "Pu-Pu Platter for 2". We then mailed away for a poster sized sheet containing dozens of Kanji symbols to choose from. Everything from Love to Diarrhea!

FYI: The symbol for good luck placed on the inner forearm (simplified, O over a sideways H) reads like the word HO when you stick your arm out to shake hands.

Aerosmith has been popular for decades. A guy had "the winged man", as Buddy referred to it, tattooed on. About 10 years later the popularity of the band had faded a bit. Same guy came in and had it covered. A few years after they got popular again. He came back in and had a new "winged man" tattoo.

807th TANK DESTROYER BATTALION

MARCH 1942 - SEPTEMBER 1945

IN MEMORY OF:

"Buddy is it you? I heard you died!" Upsetting the first time we heard this. Then about once a month we would hear it. Buddy would say, "I think my competition started that." (I think so too.) Well, it backfired. Customers would come down to see for themselves if Buddy was still there. While at the shop many of our old customers would look around and get another tattoo.

A guy named Quicko dies. Two of his friends show up from Boston with no appointment and get a small shamrock and pipe with *Quicko* under it. More friends kept showing up, by the end of the night we tattooed 12 of them.

Guy gets: "In Memory of A.G.F." It stands for, "In Memory of a Good Fuck".

A guy got a Grim Reaper with his date of birth under it and a dash. He wanted to pay us in advance to go to the funeral parlor after he dies and tattoo the death date on his arm. We couldn't take his money. Sickeningly, during WWII some Nazis had lampshades made from tattooed skin.

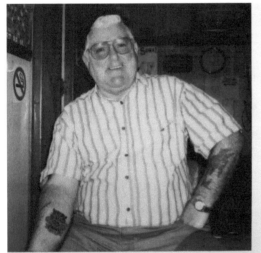

BEFORE

AFTER
BY MARILYN
1994

COVER JOBS: I only tattooed my Dad once. He had an awful old skull and cross bones done as a young soldier. He wanted it covered by his Army 807th Tank Destroyer Battalion logo. He kept leaning in to view my progress. I told him he was one of the worst customers I had worked on in a long time. He got his head out of my way and from the smile in the picture I think he was pleased.

The night I got my 1st tattoo Dad did go home and told Mom. She never had any tattoos and I was years more than old enough. Mom supposedly said, "No more!". We were all trying to figure out if that meant no more tattoos for me or no more sex for Buddy.

I saw a guy recently standing behind me in a store checkout line. He was very tattooed and I noticed he had a couple of ours on his arms.

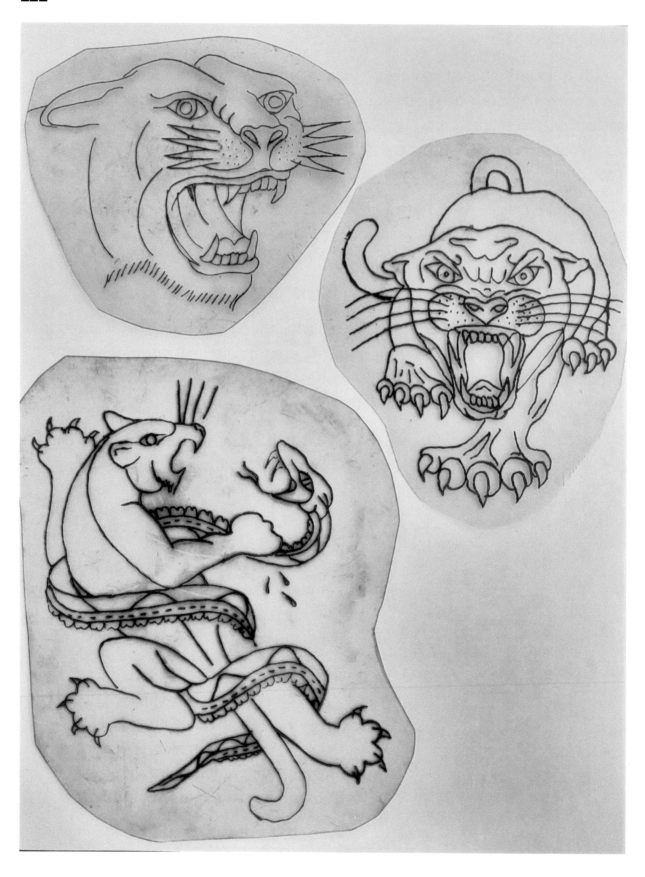

When I asked if there were more from Buddy he said pointing, "There is another under here, about 4 deep". Guy either ran out of room or kept changing his mind.

TIP: When covering a tattoo keep in mind only black truly covers black. Creative shading and darker colors with highlights disguise the rest. Design a cover job so the eyes and the mouth of the new design are over a spot with nothing under it.

As a guy is having 1 name covered, he's adding another! He said, "Fall off a woman and get right back on."

Our 1st request for large Old English writing arched above the stomach was for the word ABRASIVE. He thought he was all that. He asked, "Have you done that before?" My answer was, "NO, but we have done INSANITY and have covered HOMOCIDAL." He left.

Only a couple of times a guy came in to get his club colors covered. Buddy started and front door opened up again and a large quiet guy stood at the glass and watched. When the new outline was on and the shading begun, the cover job was well underway. The big guy said, "Have a good night", turned around and left.

A guy comes in and says, "I need a name covered." He lifts his sleeve to reveal 2 hearts and 2 names: Sue and Flo. He points to Sue. He tells me that his real name is Floramundo as he rolls his eyes he says, "Do you want to know what it means?" "Flowers of the World." "My whole name is Floramundo Andrade Duart Ferriera". His brother Manny considers himself lucky. The Mom's first name is Belvira.

A guard at a Mass prison had a homemade tattoo on his hand that we covered with a pig - "That's what they call me."

A guy asks to leave a little room under his girlfriend's name he is about to get tattooed. "If she leaves me, I'm goin' to come back and have you write SUCKS".

A Sailor wanted a chain around his ankle and "Chained to the Sea." Buddy thought he said, "Chained to the seat" and that is what he got. The sailor went bull shit. A black star over the t corrected the problem. (Write it down first).

A guy covered his 3 adopted kids names like it was nothing. Spite is a rotten thing.

EXPRESSIONS:

"See you next pay day" was Buddy's standard response to the sailors as they left the shop.

One of the nicest things about my Father was that he was a man of his word. If any one of his family or friends asked for a hand with something, "Just say the word" was his response.

One night a guy referred to me as his EXTERIOR DESIGNER. Better than the guy who asked me late one night if I was going home early because I had pulled the broom out. Don't call me a witch before it's your turn…

Then it became punk to put a tattoo on your arm but cool on the leg. The night a guy who liked his new tattoo told Buddy that the tattoo looked "BAD", Buddy was all upset. BAD! Thinking he may be saying this because he doesn't plan on paying… BAD meant good…then there was Bad Ass… Groovy, Rad, Killa, Dope…

Buddy took it upon himself to change lettering on the flash for the popular tattoo "Saturday Night's Alright for Fightin" to "Saturday Night's Alright for Lovin" and most guys would go along with it after he explained guys would come back after getting the fightin' version of the tattoo saying they had gotten in a bunch of fights because of it, (we actually covered a few). Don't tell Elton John… my Father the peace keeping romantic!

BUDDY-ISMS:

Doing a skull that had all the teeth, Buddy would remark, "Must have died young, he's got all his teeth."

Buddy liked to accent his ship tattoos with simple V shaped outlines of 2 seagulls in the distance. He would ask the Navy guys if they wanted, "a couple of Navy turkeys in the background." If you were one of the many Portuguese fishermen we tattooed he would ask them if they wanted, "a couple of Portuguese eagles."

There is an inscription on the top of crucifixes that reads, INRI. It translates to Jesus, King of the Jews. When a customer would ask what it stood for he would say, "IN Rhode Island", and we were.

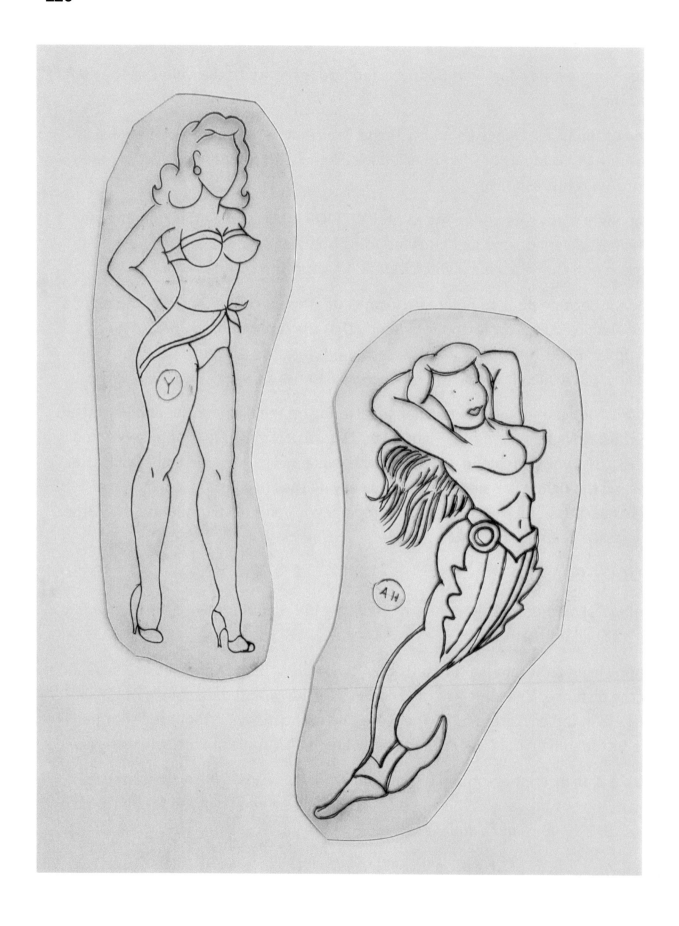

"Would you like a boy panther or a girl panther?" (or any animal really) He was hoping for the answer "What's the difference?" Then he would say "If you don't know by now I'm not going to tell you. Ask your parents when you get home".

HANDS:

Buddy thought the old TV game show <u>What's My Line</u> would have been easier for the judges if they got to examine the hands of the contestants. Pre-gloves we never fully got the ink out from under our fingernails.

Did you ever notice most old tattoo designs made it a point to have the hands hidden from view and the feet had shoes or boots on? It was a time saver and a lot less hassle drawing fingers and toes.

...SAID A CUSTOMER:

On the phone: "I'd like to place an order. I mean can I make an appointment."

"You can't hurt me, I have a high <u>quality</u> for pain."

"All of my tattoos are drawn on special, none of that lick me – stick me shit."

I asked a customer a simple question, "Where are you from?" The guy said, "The gang rape capital of the world, New Bedford (Massachusetts). I live near the bar Big Dan's. (1983, 2 or 3 guys took turns raping a woman on the pool table. The other guys who stood around and watched all got deported). The trial was broadcast live on local TV! Never before had we seen anything like this on afternoon network television! Then he asked me if I saw the write up in Hustler (Magazine). He takes another look at me and said, "I guess you probably didn't".

"I'm an urban domestic" bragged one woman.

"I'm trying not to bleed."

A guy said, "I'm going to get some Novocain next time." Buddy answers, "What and spoil all my fun?"

Customer: "Are you serious?" (another popular phrase of the time)

Standard answer "No, I'm Buddy."

Tattoos done properly do bleed a little but not much. Dad says to a customer "You don't bleed much." He replies, "I only bleed for my Shepherd (Jesus)." There were a couple of customers Buddy would mutter to me when they came in, "Get the bucket to hang off his arm", because they bled so much.

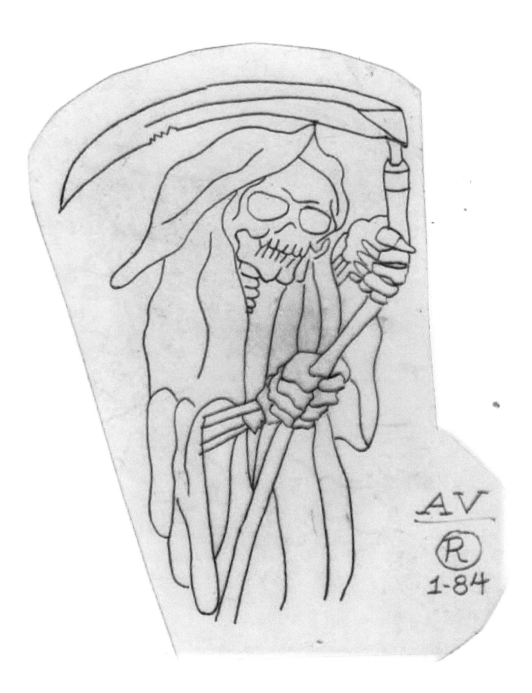

AV
®
1-84

I want: "Banker by Day – Biker <u>at</u> Night" tattooed on my arm. (Can you guess what he did for a job?)

A guy called to make an appointment. His name is Mark Bolyrenjo. He said, "Let me spell that for you M- A- R- K."

A guy is getting a stick man tattooed. He told us he likes the old, simple cave drawings. Two guys walk in and head over to the glass to see what's going on. I hear one say to the other, "I don't much care for that modern art."

Crowds went to the annual St. Patrick's Day Parade in the morning. They drank all day and came to the shop that night! We did some shamrocks if they sobered up enough. Alcohol does thin the blood. There was a biker bar called Stroker's in town for a few years with donated bras on clothes lines hanging from the ceiling. The Health Department made them take it down and wash them! A drunk girl had just gotten a bumper sticker from there. She read it to us as she acted it out, or tried to, "All I want between my legs is a Harley or a guy who owns one."

One of Buddy's expressions, when a guy or gal would come in with large jewelry, "I'd hate to fall overboard with that on." Some things you feel the need to say something about and many expect it. More than some of the time Dad's comments weren't compliments.

Two guys burst into the shop all wound up. (I'm thinking couple of jokers.) They are college age and pull out a playing card. They've come for matching Jokers, one each on the arm. I was right!

A guy gets a Reaper and wants "Doomed to Die" under it. Dad thought he said, "Doomed Today". The guy did look doomed.

A customer asks: "I want to get my wife's name Squeeze with no E."

A guy is not happy that he can't have a smoke while being tattooed. Buddy had quit smoking a few years before that. You could smoke in the waiting room (just a couple of feet away) but not while getting tattooed anymore. The guy is bragging that he does everything while having a cigarette. Has his coffee, eats his meals, while taking a piss...everything. He said even during sex!

Another smoking story: A girl tells us she met the guy sitting in the chair being tattooed only 2 days ago. She was standing in the waiting area and was going to have a cigarette. Her comment, "Oh I hope he doesn't get mad. He doesn't let me light my own cigarette!"

A girl comes in with a really drunk guy. She is very nice and sober. She tells us she wants his name covered. As she points to the name surrounded by red scars she said, "Sliced me up pretty good when we broke up." He seemed annoyed she was getting his name covered. He was her ride!

Guy brought in a bumper sticker he was thinking about getting. Glad we were booked solid. "Jeffrey Dahmer says tattoos taste great." We would have refused him if we didn't have any customers!

Girl in chair. Buddy says, "Sit still and don't move a muscle." She said, "What's a muscle?"

Question Buddy asked a customer getting a tattoo of a sexy looking girl, "Do you want me to make this a brunette?" The answer, "NO, I want brown hair!"

We heard a waiting customer point out to his friend the NO BOZOS IN THE SHOP sign. His friend said, "It's says NO BOOZE! " I like them both.

A very proud new Dad comes in to get his 1st born son's name. I sign him in and his first name is Dan. I asked what his son's name is and he got upset. "DAN OF COURSE!" I said, "Well you have Bill tattooed on your knuckles!" He said, "USED to say KILL, I changed it to BILL"...

Guy won't sit still. Buddy tells him it's like trying to tattoo a moving target. Buddy then says, "Relax, you're fighting me." The tattoo is finally finished, the guy goes to pay and says, "Here's your combat pay Buddy."

Guy (with a few drinks in him) watching his friend get tattooed coughs and blew coffee all over the customer. Dad was pissed at Mr. NO Manners. Buddy said to him, "Did your Mother have any children?" His quick comeback: "Yeah but none of them lived."

A very proud Italian young man comes in to get an Italian flag with Italia under it. "My Dad is 100% Italian. My Mom is ½ Italian. I'm going to marry a 100% Italian girl and our kids will be 100% Italian."

A girl was getting 2 cherries on her hip. Another girl in the shop about to get a tattoo asks her, "What hurt more - getting or losing your cherry?"

"I'm 1% religion and 9% Portuguese." (What happened to the other 90%?)

BUDDY'S IDEA OF THE WEIRDEST TATTOOS HE'S DONE:

Usually when asked that question Buddy would say that he had been tattooing so long what may seem weird to some doesn't faze him anymore.

Sailor comes in and Buddy notices he isn't wearing any socks. Buddy asks, "Where's your socks?" The sailor answers, "You're going to make them." He wants his ankles tattooed black. He said he didn't like wearing socks and got tired of being written up since socks are part of the uniform.

There was the Boston cabbie that had gotten held up several times. He wanted bullet holes tattooed on him.

1960's A local hooker, Carol, enjoyed bringing sailors in the shop to get her name tattooed on them. Dad said he remembered doing at least 14 of them.

Navy tattoo: A propeller on each cheek for speed. AKA Twin screws!

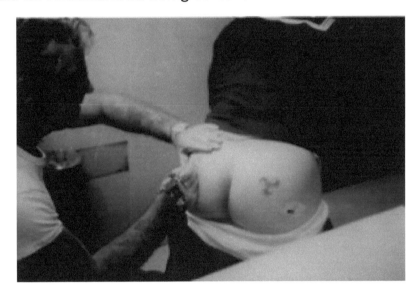

A guy and his friend come in. One says he lost a bet. He is supposed to get a ham sandwich tattooed on his leg, with a bite taken out of it. Buddy sends the guys up the street to buy one. After the sandwich is sketched and tattooed the customer, now hungry, turns to eat his sandwich and it's gone. His friend ate it!

The loser of another bet got a Skippy Peanut Butter Jar.

Lettering: "Cut along the dotted line." A guy had that tattooed just below a series of dotted lines that wrapped completely around the base of his neck.

Lettering tattooed in the middle of a guy's back: STICK KNIFE HERE (and an arrow pointing to the spot).

HEARING AIDS:

My mom got hearing aids and a battery needed replacing. We brought them with us to the shop. Dad changed out the battery then accidently dropped it. To make sure it was still working he placed it in his ear and said, "Say something." A guy who stopped in for a visit moved his mouth without a sound. HA HA everybody's a comedian. (We realized the hearing aids initially weren't working right when my Mom said to my husband, heading for KOSOVO with the Army for many months... "THE POCONOS?!" If he was heading for the Poconos on a military mission that would have been a problem!) Minutes after fixing Mom's hearing aids a guy walked into the shop and asked for a blue shark. Buddy says, "A flu shot?"

TATTOO REMOVAL (or attempting to):

Almost everything has tried to remove a tattoo - Mother's milk, goat's milk, salt and a wire brush, hydrogen peroxide, lemon juice and turpentine to name a few. The results and the amount of scaring would vary. Some homemade tattoos were deeper in the skin. The early Laser could burn out some or lots of the melatonin in the skin leaving the treated area unable to tan. One guy had a ram's head tattoo removed with repeated laser sessions. The white patch left on his arm was in the shape of a ram's head. He had us tattoo a better-looking ram's head back on! Lasers have come a long way.

ADVICE:

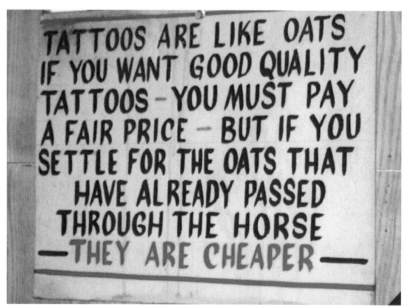

We had the prices marked on the flash. This avoided having a customer have to ask. Some were shy and some didn't want to be embarrassed if they didn't have quite enough cash with them. You could come in, look around and come back with the right amount. (ATM's weren't a thing yet.) Buddy thought it was <u>so stupid</u> (another phrase he didn't care for) when artists said to interviewers, like big shots, "I charge $100 an hour." That was lots of money 40 plus years ago. (Send a copy of that article to the tax man.)

What a bargain, especially for a chest piece!

Well maybe not - in the early 1950's.

Our lending policy sign posted in the shop said, "THE MAN WHO GIVES CREDIT IS OUT COLLECTING." (My favorite sign in the shop was: "PLEASE DO NOT FEED OR TEASE THE NON-TATTOOED PEOPLE.") Others signs read; "TATTOOS WHILE YOU WAIT," "IN GOD WE TRUST, ALL OTHERS PAY CASH," and "MY BORN LOSER TATTOO GOT INFECTED". There was also the sign he painted of a cartoon pig and the phrase, "Credit? SURE! IN A PIG'S ASS!" Buddy loved that sign and said when he wrote a book that was going to be the title. I was on board with the things he said and did but never could figure that one out. If we were a bank maybe... He did play lender, pawn shop style, many times.

When doing a large back piece, we would do them over the slower winter months. We would ask the guy about how much he wanted to spend that night. If we weren't busy and the guy was pleasant, we'd keep going.

Haggling over the price: Buddy didn't like when a guy would say, "I'll give you X amount for that tattoo." He would reply, "You'll give me nothing." If a guy said, "Buddy I'm a little short..." If we weren't busy the guy was invited to come sit in

the chair. A real character one slow winter night was with some friends that were all getting tattoos. He said he didn't have any money and really wanted a tattoo, something, anything. Dad tattooed our business card on his shoulder...

FREE ADVERTISING!

I remember a guy, much in need of a shower and always stinking like booze, would come in with his bicycle, watch for a few minutes, then leave. One rainy night, in he comes, and asks Buddy for 5 bucks. I said to myself there is no way he is going to do that. I was right and wrong. He gave the guy $10 !!! When the guy left Dad said, "He won't be back. He now owes me." We never saw him again.

CUSTOMERS COMMENTS:

A line from the movie Steel Magnolias: The nicest thing I could say about her is that her tattoos were spelled correctly. One night a guy said to another after a group of girls had just left the shop, "You could tell they were classy girls. Their tattoos were spelled right."

Buddy asked yet another gal if she wants the battleship tattooed across her chest and another customer in the shop said, "More like a dingy" …

A young lady's instructions to us, "I don't want cute blood drops."

There were 5 gals all well over 250 pounds each. One got a devil on her ribs and felt faint (OH NO) when she tried to bend over to get her head lower that her heart to feel better the tattoo disappeared. After they left the next customer said, "If tattoos were 50 cents a pound, Buddy, you could have retired tonight".

In 1980 at 23 years old when I started with Dad, I would get asked regularly, "Is that your Dad?"

In 1990 at 33 years old I was asked, "Is that your husband?" Say what?!!!

In 1996 Buddy was 72 and a guy asked me, "Is that your brother?"
HIS TATTOO WILL NEVER FADE!

Blink twice:

An 18-year-old comes in to get his first tattoo. He tells me I tattooed his name on his dad when he was born!

ANOTHER HAPPY CUSTOMER:

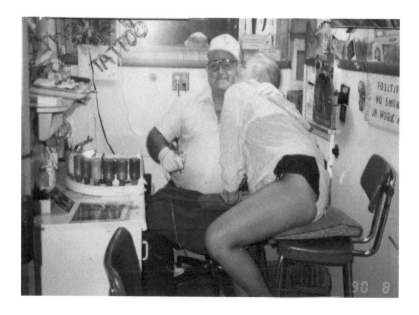

AWARDS AND LIFETIME MEMBER OF: (these are a few I know about)

Can't leave out Grandpa Groovy

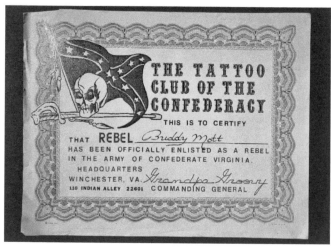

Paul Rogers and Buddy taken around 1982.

We all have people in our lives that we look up to, have taught us valuable lessons and influenced us. The smile on Buddy's face shows the true respect he had for Paul.

BOB SHAW AWARD
40 YEARS OR MORE IN TATTOOING

ABOVE FROM LEFT TO RIGHT; TWO OF BOB'S SONS – LARRY SHAW, BOBBY SHAW JR, PHOTO OF BOB BY RICHARD TODD, AND LARRY SHAW JR. BOB'S GRANDSON.

BOB SHAW AWARD RECIPIENT FOR 1994
BUDDY MOTT - 45 YEARS TATTOOING
NEWPORT, RHODE ISLAND

NATIONAL TATTOO ASSOCIATION MARCH/APRIL 1994

1994 CELEBRATING: Buddy being awarded the National Tattoo Association's Bob Shaw Award. Party pictured here was at Shakespeare's Tavern, Warren, RI.

CUSTOMER APPRECIATION PARTIES:

Fun to get a group together. They all had our tattoos in common. We knew them but they didn't know each other until that day. Plenty to show and talk about. Almost half came on bikes, some traveling from and hour or two away. We were going to take a group shot inside the rather large bar Gillary's in Bristol, RI, BUT there wasn't enough room for that, so outside we went. A few of the guys with big backpieces had taken their shirts off. Before we all ended up in the road I said, "Up against the wall" and this is what I got...

1998 CELEBRATING 50 YEARS IN BUSINESS

Buddy with some fellow tattoo artists at the party.

SOME KEPT IT INTERESTING, IT TAKES ALL KINDS

1987-ish, 2 guys came in - the one with no tattoos said to his friend, "I'm not getting a tattoo. Your body is a temple." The tattooed guy said, "Yeah, and these are the stained glass windows."

Guy has tattooed on forearm: AMERICAN MADE

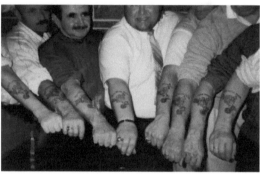

The Blue Knights is a large group of Police Motorcycle Riders.
Their emblem is a Knight on a horse with the front legs raised in the air and a bike wheel at the bottom. The guys would come five at a

time and all get the same design. The mouth on the horse is slightly open. One night a guy getting the tattoo never stopped talking, not for a second. Buddy realized only when it was done, that he had made the mouth on that guy's horse closed.

Bob & Betty Ames

This photo was taken in 1978, 2 years before I met the Ames. I learned quick when you saw the names Bob & Betty on the appointment sheet it was going to be a great night. They would come down on the bikes and bring family and friends, lots of them. The ride was over an hour from Middleboro, MA, and some summer nights they rode back in some pretty heavy fog. Bob was a bike builder/mechanic at Monty's and Bettencourt's and past President of the MC Tumbleweeds. He went on to get several tattoos. Two extra special ones are pictured near the end of the book.

A gal said she has 10 toes and wants a flower on each toe. Then she couldn't make up her mind between the toes, or the Chinese symbol for health or witch... so she got the symbol for child instead.

Request for a dead tree on the back of one leg and a live tree on the other leg.

Request: "Do you have Bugs Bunny in drag?" Buddy replied, "We could slap a dress on it."

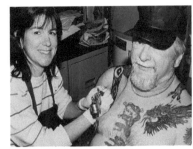

More happy customers.

A wise guy wanted lettering in Chinese. He was hoping people would ask him what it stood for. The translation was: "If I tell you, you'll know".

The Blues Brothers names became popular. We tattooed several - JAKE on one inner wrist and ELWOOD on the other.

We tattooed a nurse, often. First, she got a huge Pegasus on her back. She then would bring in drawings her young daughter had done of kitties and doggies. She got ALL of them tattooed on herself. Pam was a dedicated animal owner with approx. 30 cats and 5 dogs (no furniture) on the 1st fl. of the 2 unit apartment building she owned and only 5 cats and 2 dogs upstairs with her. I can only imagine walking by at night and all those eyes would be looking at you out the windows.

We did work on many members of the 'Red Hat Society'. Ladies turning 50 and most getting their first tattoo. (1990's) They talked a lot but were always entertaining.

A tattoo of a worn human heart with a patch for her young daughter's upcoming heart operation (later we heard the operation was a success).

Civilian wants, "Beechwood aged" above the belly button and under it: "On tap here."

Buddy did many "Sweet and Sour" or "Hot & Cold" over the nipples...

And then there was Tom Davis a well-known character in Newport. He would tell people he had his eye on you as he lifted his shirt to reveal the tattooed face on his rather large gut. The mouth was his belly button.

One night he stopped in for a visit. Tom showed a customer sitting in the chair being tattooed his "face". According to my notes her name was Suzi with an "i". She had bright blond hair and was squirming and complaining about how much the multi-colored lizard she was having tattooed was hurting. She said to Tom, "That face tattoo must have hurt!" His reply, "No, I've got no brain." The punch line was her response, "Then I must be wicked smart cause this is killing me."

Pre-phone at the shop: One night we get to the shop and find 2 post-it notes on the door. "Additional thoughts over my earlier letter" was on one and the second had 2 boxes checked READ and REVIEW WITH ME. I called the number and "…maybe I want a big fly and 2 smaller flies on my shoulder…" We then checked the DISCARD box instead. Inside a letter is on the floor, no postage, dropped off thru the mail slot in the door. It is from another guy. Very detailed of what he has tattooed and a list of about 15 things he may get one of someday. As we read on, all he really wanted to know was our hours. We considered ourselves lucky we missed them both!

During the 70's the drinking age dropped to 18. (Fun for me growing up then.) A few years later the drinking age was back to 21. In about 2001 an 18-year-old came in with proper ID and his Mother. She was nice enough and rolled her eyes at me once when he wasn't looking. He thought he was Mr. Big Shot, Know-It-All. So annoying! He was heading off to Freshman year at college in a few weeks. At some point I was fed up and looked at him and told him I felt sorry for him. I said, "When I was 18, the drinking age was 18 and sex wasn't going to kill you." His Mom nodded and smiled.

A couple called and made an appointment. Two for Saturday. "We're getting married Saturday. Our reception is in Connecticut so we probably won't be there until 11:30 p.m." WHAT? Second thought, "NO PROBLEM" I said. Why argue. They won't show up. I wrote their names down on the pad anyway. Sure enough, Saturday came and straight from the reception they arrived. They said they stayed pretty sober because they knew they were driving an hour to Newport and getting tattoos!

One night there was a car horn that beeped outside the shop. Dad said, "Go check that out, I think that's your Mother." (That's as close to a visit as Mom would get to the shop.) I put my machine down, took the gloves off and out I go. Yes, it's Ma. She was on her way to some kind of classical music concert in Newport and one of her choir members was in the car too. Her friend wanted to see where the shop was. I wished them a nice time at the show and told them I've got to get back

inside because we are crazy busy. I'm headed back to my work area and I can't believe what I'm looking at. The guy I left sitting there for no more than 3 minutes had picked up the tattoo machine and was tattooing himself! I asked, "What are you doing?" He put the machine back on the counter. I still couldn't believe it. When I sat back down I told him not to do that again and gave his hand a quick slap - old school. We both laughed.

A night in the 70's and a guy wanted Buddy to do a tattoo without a stencil or pen sketch, not even making 1 reference mark to go by. They discussed a few ideas. Buddy was about to begin and looked up to see that the famous tattoo artist Paul Rogers had just walked thru the door. My father said he was honored Paul came to the shop. The customer with no markings on his arm is sitting in the chair ready. Dad said he took a breath and tattooed his favorite, a square-rigged sailing ship under full sail. He told me proudly that Paul really liked it and was impressed with how little time it took.

Half-way thru a Marine Corps tattoo, to make conversation, Buddy would ask the question, "Where did you do your boot?" Once the guy said he was leaving next week for basic training. We didn't bother to tell him that was the dumbest thing he could have done. We're sure he was worked 10 times + harder than any other private. Buddy started to ask the, "Where did you do your boot?" question first.

A couple comes in, mentions they are dating and the skinny guy gets: "MAX CAP 125 lbs." tattooed in good size letters on his lower stomach with an arrow pointing down. All fine and dandy, but the gal he was with was 300 lbs. easy!

 A TV show announced one night that Michael Jackson had just married Lisa Marie Presley. The show Current Affair referred to them as Newly Weirds...Buddy chimed in that he agreed with that. Another customer brought up that the sweet actress Valerie Bettinelli had recently married a rock star but the guy can't remember which one. Dad thought Valerie was cute. Buddy says without hesitation, "Van Halen." I was shocked! I said to the customers listening, "He couldn't name the 4 Beatles on a bet or where they are from, for any amount of money." Guy in the shop answers, "They're from Liverpool, England." Buddy then says to me, "Your Great Grandfather was from Liverpool." WHAT?! **WOW**

A guy gets the name "Hendrix" on the left inner forearm facing up so he can read it and on the other arm the Chinese symbol "to play music" tattooed sideways.

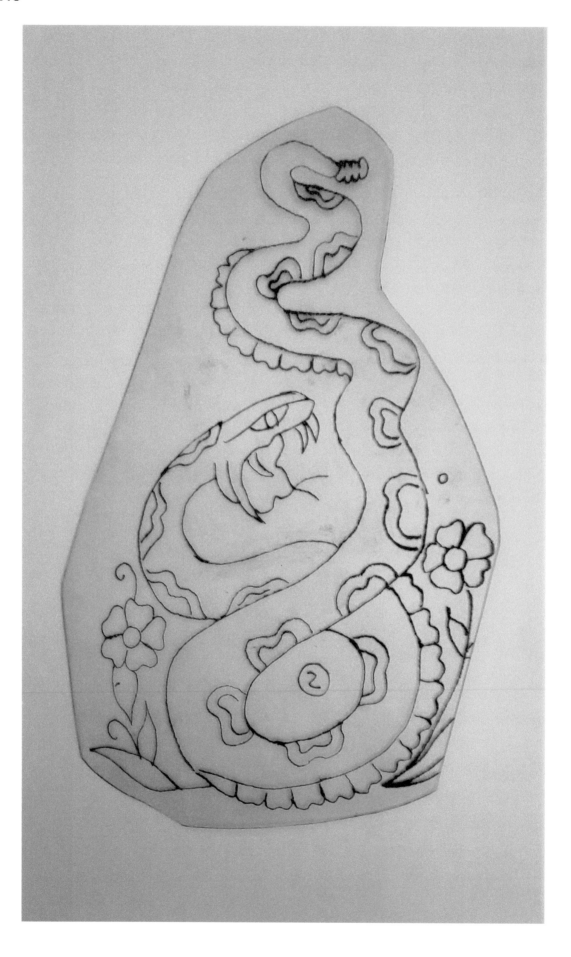

It is difficult to tattoo a round circle on a curved cheek of the ass. Buddy tattooed many U.S. GOVERNMENT GRADE A INSPECTED stamps, always on the butt. Years ago a 'lady' was making a statement when she asked for and got this particular tattoo. Just a few years ago my Father had a roommate at the Veteran's Home. We heard all about this guy's girlfriend but never met her until one afternoon in she came. She seemed street wise around the edges. She couldn't believe Buddy was there and was happy to see him. Drum roll... "You tattooed me back in the day. I got the Grade A stamp on my ass."

I fell for the T-shirt with the 1/8th inch print. I was signing in a guy and I leaned in to looked closer. It said, "What are you looking at the fuckin' nosey bitch?"

A guy gets a heart and a knife with his wife's name in the banner. "If she wants to cut my heart out, I'll give her something to do it with."

Early 90's a gay guy wants a small devil with "Bitch" written under it. After the tattoo he said, "Can I take a Stop & Shop Ibuprofen now?" Love those guys..

Preppie Frat brothers came in for matching tattoos of a SKI MOG on the leg. It was a Gremlin lookin' thing chewing a ski pole in the teeth. They wanted the teeth stained yellow/brown. (Another old 80's expression Preppie. Clean cut, golf style shirt, boat shoes and no socks.)

A few customers with little warning will get sick to their stomachs. Dad never ate pineapple pie again after his experience. I went years holding off on eating clam chowder. I had done a craft fair in downtown Newport on a Saturday with my sister. I make personalized nautical shell ornaments (The Handy Dandy Boat Company). The snack bar said just another minute for the batch of chowder to be ready. They said this 3 times. That was going to be my dinner. I couldn't wait any longer and had to get to the shop for 6 p.m. I arrive at 6:10 and the shop is in full swing. Dad, shaking his head and with a disgusted look, tells me to "Go check out the guy in the bathroom." As I approach the door a pale guy is coming out. He threw up clam chowder all over the wall of the bathroom. No apology. When he felt better, I made him clean it!

The lady wrapped in snake tattoos is back...

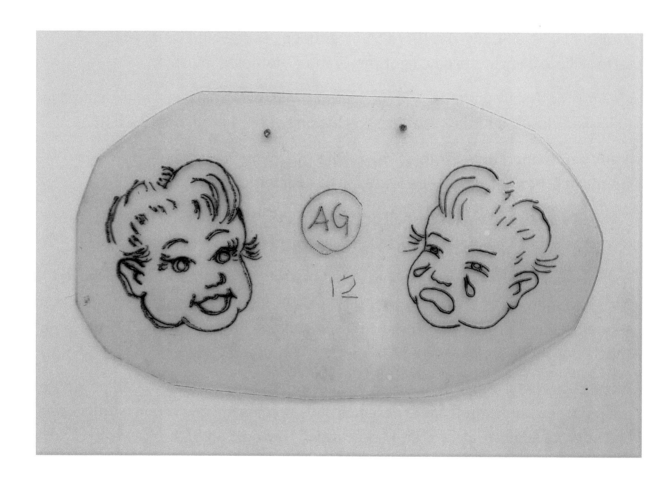

"Should I get Underdog white or light brown?" This customer is taking a vote from strangers in the shop…

"Do you have skin color ink?" (Can't get more skin color than your own skin!)

Pigs were popular. A girl's request: "I'd like a pig doin' a back flip on the cheek of my ass".

"I want comedy and <u>calamity</u> masks."

The show Jeopardy is on the TV. The question was, "Name the 2 countries in Africa that used to be known as Portuguese West Africa and Portuguese East Africa." At least 40 percent of our customers were Portuguese. A customer from Fall River yells the answer out, "Fall River and New Bedford." Pretty funny considering those are small cities, not countries and in Massachusetts located about a half an hour up the road. (The answer was Angola and Mozambique).

3 guys on bikes coming down from Massachusetts one night got pulled over. They were doing 85 in a 65 and had small helmets on, not legal in Rhode Island. The cop asked, "Is that a helmet or a candy dish and where are you headed?" The guy said, "Candy dish Sir and heading to Buddy's." They got let go with a warning.

A customer asks for a cupcake and his initials…and a cherry with a stem over his heart. (With a straight face he tells us his initials are F.A.G.) If my son was named after my Dad's Dad, Samuel Allen, his initials would have been S.A.S. If we named him Allen Samuel and our last name then began with an S the initials would have been A.S.S.! Who wants to go thru life with the initials ASS. A tattoo artists friend had a baby name picked out. The first name Owen after the famous tattoo artist Owen Jensen. Just before delivery they decided to go with Michael instead of Steven for the middle name. They realized later his initials are O.M.G.

The guy with his banana yellow thong had chain we tattooed, section at a time, wrapped around most of his body. Somehow along the way he got a girlfriend, and she wanted chain like him! Chain guy then wanted a chain around his privates. (Once again old Navy regulations came in handy.) We sent him to New Hampshire.

A guy got a vicious looking Doberman with his 2 daughters names below. The wife said, "You forgot me!" He said, "No I didn't, you're looking at it" as he points to the snarling dog tattoo.

152

Buddy always calling most of the guys Skip… Up next a guy wanted the Anheuser-Busch eagle and Budweiser written under it. The license says Janet and someone in the shop called her Janet. I try to get Dad's attention, too late, "Hey Skip what will you have?" I chime in, "Janet would like…" we needed better signals. Another night a guy came in who was very tall and had a baseball cap on. The request was for a small tattoo of a teddy bear on the shoulder. Hunter was the name, NO hint there. The cap came off the hair flowed down and she was a stunning looking person who modeled for a living.

Upside down smiley face with "Round 2 It" He said, "Cause someday, I'm going to get Round to it."

Sad commentary on some classless folks who tattooed. A young girl came in one night and wanted to get another tattoo on her ankle. She started to take her pants off. I was surprised and told her she didn't need to get undressed. She told me the guy that did the first one made her take her pants off. That's a PIG! I heard several stories like that. Not our job to gawk, flirt, talk about your underwear, grope… (Rant over)

The Friday appointment pad page from home said, Norman 9:20 p.m. NO, NO MOM. Again, she didn't give the proper spiel: We take a handful of names and do them in the order you show up starting at 7. The closer to 7 the better, by 9 anyway. The phone rings at 9:30, "Hi it's Norman. I have a 9:20 appointment. I'm still in Framingham (2 hrs. away)." His cat got hit by a car. I try to console him and finally convince him to come Tuesday. He then calls back for more consoling! Shortly after my friend Kathy calls and always said first, "Are you busy?" I said "Norman's cat got hit by a car." She said, "Who the hell is Norman?" The next night Kathy calls and says she can't come her giraffe has whiplash. When we finally meet Norman 4 days later at his Tuesday appointment, we find out his cat was hit by a car on Thursday not Friday and the cat is now fine!

Same night as Norman…Guy wants a skull and a knife with some lettering under it: Son of Neptune. Next line: Uncle to Charlie the Tuna. Next line: 2nd Cousin to the Little Mermaid. The next customer wants a gorilla… Maybe we should all take a Stop & Shop Ibuprofen.

A lady with a couple of drinks in her is sitting next to her boyfriend who is being tattooed. She won't shut up and then tells us, "I'm dainty." Dad says, "Yeah but you've got the mouth like a bulldozer." Next, she falls off the chair and says, "I was doing aerobics".

Shop door opens and in come 2 nuns wearing the old black and white floor length habit head to toe, complete with rosary beads. Something about one of them

looked familiar. I had forgotten my friend Kathy Brownell got a part in the chorus of a local theatre's production of The Sound of Music. They were in the 1st scene and had to be back for the curtain call at the end. What better way to kill time than to hang out at the tattoo shop. Every customer was now staring at them and glancing

back at me. After doing a double take It finally clicked who she was and I said in a disgusted voice, "You again! I told you the 2 for 1 nun special ended last month." Buddy looked up confused. I said to him, "Say Hi to Sister Kathy." (The guy in the middle is a customer waiting his tattoo turn. A good sport that didn't want to pass up a photo op like this).

We did tattoo a real Nun once, that I know about. She was in town for a family wedding and had a cousin with her. She, the nun, is getting small flowers on the outside of her ankle. Now we head in my back room so I can color the design and I ask what color she would like the flowers. She said, "Light blue, the Virgin Mary's color." That's too much info, it's summer and hot... The cousin says, "Tell her." She said, "I'm a Nun." When we were finished, we headed out to the front and I asked Dad if he can guess what she does. No answer. I said, "Now you can tell my Mother you tattooed a Nun." He looked guilty. Hey wasn't our idea. She pulled out her wallet and Buddy, said "NO charge." Then he gave her a T-shirt. Til the day we closed we got mailings to donate to their convent in New York.

"I want a small eagle, globe and anchor on my hip. I'm a wimpy Marine."

Guys asking for the USMC emblem pictured on left, Buddy would joke, "You mean the seagull sitting on a beach ball with his thumb up his ass, wishing he was in the Navy?"

Robin is getting married next week. She needs Joe's name covered and she has it tattooed on her twice. She also got her fiancée's name added under the devil.

A six-foot tall, real big guy said, "I'd like an angel – a real masculine looking angel."

We did a few "Snap-on-Tools". Beyond loyal employees! We did talk the 18-year-old that just got his 1st full time job at MOVER'S WORLD out of getting MOVER'S WORLD tattooed complete with logo. We heard 2 months later he was fired!

A skier comes in and gets the Grim Reaper carrying skis over the shoulder and ski poles under the arm.

Another guy asks for the GRIN Reaper. That's up there with "Sesame Sam" and "The guy with the guns" (Can't believe guns were recently removed from Yosemite Sam and Elmer Fud!!!) We did an Elmer on a guy's butt cheek with the rifle pointing to the asshole and the lettering: "Come out of that hole you wascally wabbit." Wouldn't be the same without the gun!

Another guy asks for the: "Tamen Devil. You know, the devil with the horns and the mug of beer."

Kid comes in with his parents. Kid has a fake tattoo. Kid pulls out Bacitracin and rubs it on the fake tattoo. I admit I took a second glance to see if their approx. 10-year-old had been tattooed somewhere recently. He wasn't.

Biker comes in and wants the name Di covered up. His friend suggests just adding an ED on the end.   (DIED)

Two older biker couples come in and it's late. The husband says to the wife, "Honey, so where are you going to put it?" His biker friend says, "How about off until tomorrow" ...and we all went home.

Girl is getting a Pegasus on her hip. Buddy draws the first line. Happens to be the tail, back hip and leg. "STOP! STOP! I CAN'T!"   There is no convincing her to continue. She is probably still walking around with just a horse's ass on her hip.

Girl gets tattoo of her fiancé's name. "I can't show him this tattoo for another 45 days – he's getting out then. (vacation...) This is my sister, she's 15". Little Sis says, "That must feel worse than labor." The reply, "No, but you'll find out in 7 months."   !!!

A girl and her baby come in. She is getting a huge rose tattoo on her arm and doesn't flinch. She says, "This is nothing – when I had the baby they didn't give me anything – not even an aspirin. My birthing coach wasn't on the ball. I yelled, TAKE A PICTURE! She spazzed. I grabbed the camera and started clicking away – even the nurse couldn't believe it. I guess I can take pain."

A woman and her young 7-year-old son (with no front teeth) – before I could get the privacy curtain down the kid says, "My Mother would like privacy." Then he announces to the shop there is blood in the bathroom sink. I go check it out and there is a very small, tiny rust spot from where the faucet used to drip. Another woman in the shop told me, "The kid asked me what type of toys do my children play with?" His best announcement was as Mom was filling out the sign in card, "Mom you're not 35, you're 37!"

 Girl gets a skunk with: "Love Stinks" under it.

Self-proclaimed Princess...wants a "Silver Tiara with jewels on my ass so everyone will know I'm a Princess."

A NICE SURPRISE I CAME ACROSS: THIS EVENT/BIRTHDAY BOOK

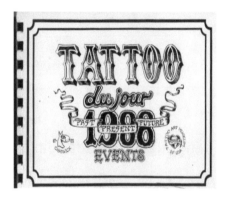

This Calendar book by Lyle and Judy Tuttle, was mailed to us. They had sent out flyers asking us to share our info. Buddy shares a page with Edward W. "Dad" Liberty of Scully Square days in Boston. Buddy & Cap Coleman Cap were both born on Oct.25th. I share a page with Tattoo Stiggy (World Record Most Tattoos, 1980), Oct.14th. (Listed then as Marilyn Mott St. Ours.)

Pictured below are just the first 2 pages of the book.

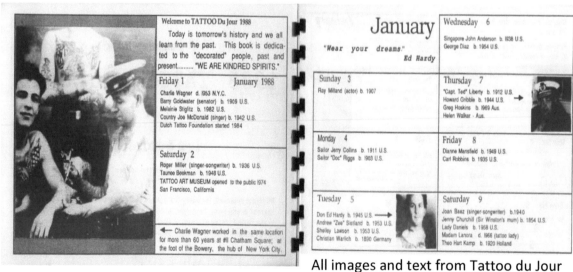

All images and text from Tattoo du Jour are the property of the Lyle Tuttle Collection and may not be reproduced without proper permissions. Thanks for letting me include this special memory.

JUST A FEW OF THE MEMORABLE CUSTOMERS:

DAN: A great photographer and collector of tattoos, AKA to us as Timbuk

He got many tattoos from us and had a distinct Long Island New York (Long Guyland, Nu- yark) accent. Over time working on him he would teach me a poetic joke his Mother had taught him including the word Timbuktu (this was over 25 years ago and wasn't written in the notes, but here goes): Two guys die at the same time and arrive at the Pearly Gates. St. Peter greets them and says, "We only have room for one. Whoever can use the word Timbuktu in a poem gets in." The 1st guy thinks a minute and says:

"While standing on burning sand
overlooking a foreign land,
a caravan came into view
it's destination Timbuktu".

St. Peter is pleased and welcomes him.
Guy #2 says, "Hey, don't I get a turn?"

"Tim and I a hunting we went.
We came upon 3 maidens in a tent.
They were 3, we were but 2,
I bucked one and Tim bucked two!" HA HA

An old tattoo joke:

Guy comes in and asks the artist to tattoo a 100-dollar bill on his penis. The artist is not thrilled and says to him, "If you can give me 3 good reasons you want that I'll think about it." Guy says, "Well, I like to play with my money. I like to watch my money grow and I want to see how fast my girlfriend can blow a hundred bucks." Drop your drawers and have a seat.

MOE The owner of the D I I K CLUB:

For years we were tattooing a bunch of local guys that all knew each other from the DIIK Club. I had been hearing about this private club for a while but wasn't sure what or where it was. Moe came in one night and asked me if Buddy and I were ever going to stop in at the DIIK (loosely pronounced Dick) Club. I asked Moe what that stood for and he said, "Damned If I Know."

I talked to Dad about it at closing. I said, "What's the worst that could happen, we won't know anybody there, we'll have a drink and leave." Shortly before last call we walked thru the door of this small building. It looked like an old fishing shack, but it wasn't near the water. Moe, (the perfect wise guy owner/ bar tender) looks up from behind the bar and says loudly, "BUDDY!" Heads turn and in unison about 20 others repeat, "BUDDY!" They can't believe he was there. It was one of the greatest nights in Dad's many years. We couldn't buy a drink. Next, Moe takes out a piece of 2x4 and taps it on the bar 3 times. (It is 5 minutes of 1 a.m.) He said, "You know what to do and you know when to do it." The whole place stands, picks up their drinks and head for the side door. "Not you Buddy" says Ingrid. We were introduced to her as his bouncer. Moe said no one was going to give that German with an 18" neck any shit. Minutes later members are coming back in to get another full beer to take outside. They say this would go on most of the night. We were given applications to be members and Ingrid explained it was $10 the first year and $5 a year every year after that. Soon after, Moe and his wife Sharon dropped our Official Membership cards off at the shop. The number on Buddy's card was 007, as in Bond, James Bond!

Several years later I invited a few of my friends to join me for a drink there at noon on New Year's Day. A few of the customers were still there from the night before, prob. sitting on the same barstool and still wearing their party clothes.

Sadly, Moe died from complications of agent orange (a defoliating chemical used in Viet Nam). He was a great guy.

Mosher family and friends, the next generation came in for some art of their own.

LULU:

"My name is Lucille, you can call me LULU. I want a moon tattooed on the side of my hip and the sun on the other hip, because the world revolves around my ass." We close the curtain. She has a sundress on. As she pulled up the dress, revealing no underwear, she said, "Buddy, I douched for you." Dad got a little red in the face. He starts, I'm standing behind her where the folding door meets the wall. At this point Dad and I had worked together for several years and we developed a slightly sarcastic joking relationship. I looked into the crowd of customers and said, "Ma!" with a surprise in my voice. (Mom never came into the shop. I thought it was funny, still do. He taught me well.) Thinking back, it's a wonder he didn't have a heart attack. LULU came back in a few weeks later. We were standing in the small crowded waiting area. To make conversation I asked, "How did the tattoos come out?" She said, "Nice". She had a sundress on and pulled it up to her waist to show me. Again, no underwear. A couple of guys in the shop looked over...She said, "What the fuck are you lookin' at!" They looked away. We heard she worked for a while on an oil barge in the Gulf. When it got hot some guys were working with their shirts off...no surprise, her too. She also had 2 close friends (Tommy with the black eye pictured here, just being himself) and when they were all in town they would meet up for drinks and a game of pool. These guys were rougher and tougher than most. Evidently 2 Puerto Ricans in the bar

didn't think they were funny. Both of LULU's friends were stabbed in the gut. As her friends lay on the floor bleeding LULU picked up a pool cue. The cops showed up to find she had knocked both of the stabbers cold. All survived.

She came in another night with a half a bottle of booze, carrying a bathing suit. She wanted the tiger face and leafy background design pictured on the bathing suit tattooed on her calf. I draw a stencil and she disappears coming out of the bathroom a few minutes later wearing just the suit. "WHAT are you lookin' at" she said while glaring at one of our waiting customers... Here we go again...

Eventually she also got a tattoo on her neck of an angel whispering in one ear and a devil in the other.

JIM, known to the Newport locals as GIMP:

Owner and operator of (as Buddy referred to it in 1995) The Flyin' Shithouse.

Gimp had a 3-wheel motorcycle with a wooden outhouse looking overhang, complete with the crescent moon cut out. He was well known in Newport. Regularly he would come visit aided by 2 canes and wearing a motorcycle jacket.

When he would leave, we told our customers he would do a wheelie. Many non-believers came outside and YES, he did a wheelie as he tore up the street. Hence

the name "Flyin' Shithouse."

Quite a sight to see!

AL & AL:

Albert and Albertina Faye were regular customers. We called them Al & Al. He was the only customer that was allowed to get 2 tattoos in one night instead of 1 per customer. His tattoos made perfect mirror images. He wouldn't sleep right if he had a design on one side and not the other. He developed a Sea theme on his chest. Started with a large Mermaid. He wanted us to change it into a King Neptune look. (We nicknamed it a Mer-man or a Man-maid). Then he had 2 small Mermaids added below, of course one on each side. (Mimi-maids)---Faye never got any tattoos. They always came in together and 1 night she bought a T-shirt for her 85 + year old Mother. They started dating when they were young, (he was older than she) got married, 6 months later got divorced and then they lived together happily after that. He loved her and beer, cold beer. (I'll share 2 tips from him: If you take a couple of beer cans to work to have with lunch, keep them hidden and chilled in the toilet tank and Tip 2: Al, if he really liked something, like a belt or wallet, would buy two. A great idea that I do to this day.) Al heard about a guy that got a pair of horseshoes tattooed on his ass like he was kicked. Right up his alley, two! Guess what we tattooed on him that night, 1 on each cheek.

CJ:

He and his motorcycle are well decorated. The bike measures 11 feet 2 inches

long! CJ would park it right in front of our small shop taking over the whole sidewalk. Cops would stick their head in, figuring it belongs to the biggest guy in the place and ask to have the bike moved across the street. One night he told the cop it was mine and I'd move it! He thought it was funny to put his arm across me and say, "Protect me, Muriel." I didn't bother to correct him, it became a running joke. He had a different M starting name for me every time, except Marilyn. He was a champion prize fighter in his earlier days. His hands are the size of pie plates. He has lots of interesting stories and tattoos to match. Examples: (just on his hands alone) an eyeball tattooed on his thumb knuckle ("I've got my eye on you"), a zipper across the knuckles on 1 hand and a tattoo of stitches on the knuckles of his other hand, Highway to Hell across the top of his right hand etc...

(NOW FROM ONE EXTREME TO THE OTHER)

A man Buddy hadn't seen in years with a good amount of tattoos wants a very large tattoo like the one on the poster he is showing us. This 40+ year old man is my size. (My license still SAYS I'm 5') He is maybe 5'2" and real skinny. He wants an eagle head – huge American flag in background, a HD emblem and "Born in the USA" on his chest, his whole chest. I think Dad is calling him Tiny but I'm not sure. I didn't call him anything – glad I didn't. His name is Piney! He came in every couple of weeks for all the outline in the winter months. The slow season, great time for a

(Guys would get the "Hey You" - "Who Me" tattooed on the back shoulders,
1 each and when standing together they lined up. We did lots of 2 part cartoons.)

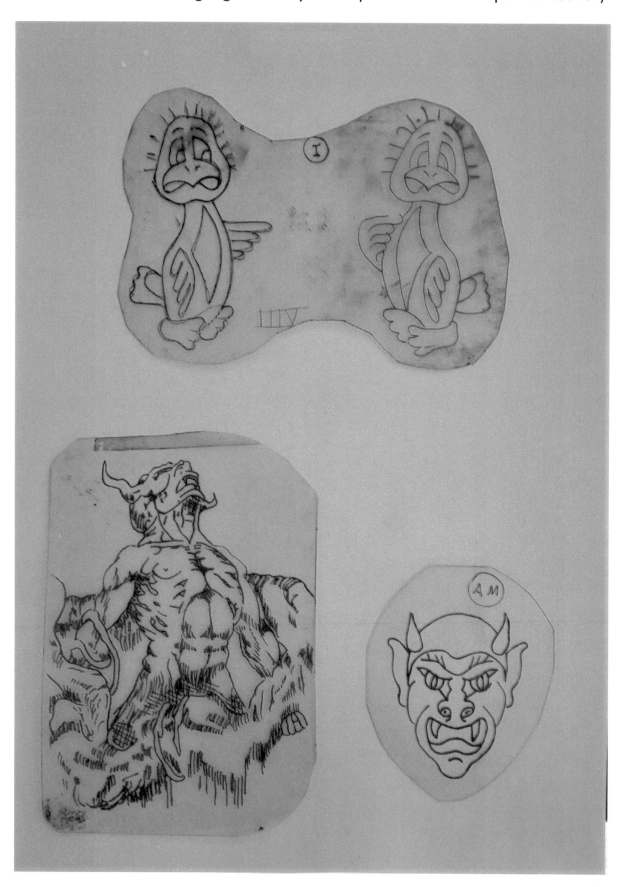

project. We had a good sized rubber skeleton from Halloween hanging up in the back room, my 'office'. We also were making a variety of pins then too. We happened to put a pin of a big American flag on the skeleton. I spotted it as he was following me in the back for color. We didn't do it to look like him but it sure did. I managed to toss something over it. He was a very nice person, Tiny or Piney...and never moved a muscle.

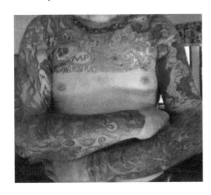

We tattooed our tall friend Scott P. many times. He continued at Inflicting Ink with a whole Vegas scene on his back and many other tats when we retired. In this day and age of people identifying as many different things he said, "I identify as illustrated."

"ALL I WANT IS A _____ ..."

It's late, we lock the door and shut most lights off at 11. We were supposed to be out by 1 a.m. but we would stay and finish nice people. The door is locked and KNOCK KNOCK. I opened the door, maybe if it's a small simple one we'll do it. "All I want is a Ying Yang with a J on each side." Sounds easy enough. He tells us he 'fell' over Niagara Falls and hung onto the rocks. It took 3 rescue guys chained together to save him. We remembered seeing that on the news! "Oh, and can you add some splashing water, the falls and a few rocks?" All I want is to go home!

The first tattoo in 1976 the Bicentennial year: "All I want is a Liberty Bell." That same year Buddy's friend, a very talented Providence tattoo artist Ronnie Daigle, entered a Bicentennial art contest sponsored by a Boston radio station. He tattooed a whole back piece of the ship Old Ironsides and the skyline of Boston Harbor behind it. Ronnie did a beautiful job and won! His prize, a pound of gold!

"All I want is a girl's name tattooed on my arm," said a sailor. "What's the name?" The answer was, "It doesn't matter. Lots of the other guys have their sweeties name on their arm and I don't have a girlfriend." Buddy said, "How about Alice?"

"All I want is 2 pieces of plywood on my arm." Guy shows me 2 squares of paper he drew of plywood showing the grain. "Well, one square will go horizontal, the other vertical..."I knew there was more..."The 2 directions represent the cross," on and on. He asked a price. I turned to Dad and said, "What's it cost for a couple of sheets of plywood?" Buddy's answer, "What kind?" That was a long night.

"All I want is Snoopy driving backwards." In the same night another said, "All I want is a tiger with no eyes."

"All I want is MOM tattooed on my ass, when I stand on my head it'll say WOW." Back in the day *Mother* was spelled out in banners. Just 1 guy asked for "**MA**".

"All I want is a skull on my back. Well, it's a lady looking into a mirror and it looks like a skull from a distance, and did I mention I want a horseshoe of roses framing it?" We did this 'All Is Vanity' project in sessions. Doug Eaton was no stranger to big tattoos, sat still and was a pleasure to work on. He drove over 2 hours one way. I had this picture up on the wall over my work station for years. The green dots are from mixing color one night that did the air pocket release, twice! Splat! The picture started to turn green, and of course, so did I.

You never knew what to expect when the Silveira's came in. "All I want is a Ying

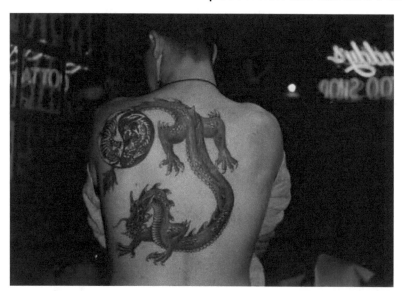

Yang made up of a tiger and a black dragon, and a large dragon to cover most of my back, not all tonight." We could hear Joe, Mike's Dad pull up on his scoot. Joe had all his grandchildren's names tattooed with designs he thought up. They were all very nice and very different, all the names started with the letter M. (Even his son's family dog's name, that he didn't have tattooed, started with an M). A kind heart and a generous soul. If a cause or a need arises, Joe is your man.

"All I want is a golf club with a mohawk hair do, smoking a cigar, wearing oval sunglasses..."

"All I want is a trigger housing on the inside of my leg."

"All I want is a Pegasus and AGGRA in big letters under it." He feels the need to tell us it is for all the aggravation in his life.

"All I want is the Eisenhower symbol on my chest." I'm not familiar with that one, so I ask the guy to describe it to me. Then I caught on, he wants the Anheuser A with the eagle and Budweiser written under it!

"All I want is 2 eagles connected at the talons doin' it."

"All I want is my wife's name on my arm and she said to write MY WIFE above it."

"All I want is 2 alligators on my chest, like the Izod shirt, doin' it doggie style."

"All I want is a monkey on my back."

"All I want is a horseshoe on my ass where my horse kicked me."

"All I want is a Chuanastarcloud. It's a cloud made out of stars representing infinite beauty." So she said.

"All I want is the bar code from a pack of Marlboro reds." Back then (early 1980's) the lines were on the side of the packs but they weren't being used for scanning yet. Not many people even knew what they were for.

"All I want is a shark wearing a bandana and glasses, playing the guitar with a cord plugged into a socket in my armpit."

"All I want is to pay you to run a dry (without ink) needle across my back." NO! Almost reminded me of the creepy guy with no tattoos that would sit and watch his wife get one small tattoo after another on her rather large breasts as she carried on wincing in pain.

"All I want is the Recycling symbol." (Buddy said he looked more like hazardous waste.)

"All I want is an ant on my chest ½" high and 1" long", said the young lady. "It has to have red eyes. Buddy you can make the eyes red, right?" He said, "We're here to please." (Well, most of the time.)

Let's call him Antony, "All I want is a Tic Tac Toe board on my ass", said a Catholic high school senior working on a film project.

"All I want is a turtle laying on his back with a quilt and fuzzy slippers."

"All I want is a Ying Yang and 2 fish. Yellow and red – but, I don't want it to look like McDonald's colors... (I was thinking Mc Ying Yang!)

"All I want is a black belly button."

"All I want is a bird pulling a worm out of my belly button." (Used to be popular with the Sailors.)

"All I want is a large fruit basket tattooed on my ass. It has to have some grapes and a couple of bananas..." After a few sessions to complete, it came out really nice. She made us a handmade thank you gift! A farm stand style, hand painted fruit basket with the lettering below: "Buddy's Produce Market."

"All I want is 702." He claimed it was the code in prison for insane.

An insistent gal started her request with **I'm getting** a large Praying Mantis between my shoulders. She felt the need to tell me, with a glint in her eye, that after sex the female bites the head right off the male. She left out the part about then devours his corpse for nourishment! (Every mother's dream for their son...)

A guy, 6 foot 6" and 350 pounds; "All I want is a small submarine periscope on my chest. I want the top to show just above my V- neck shirts."

Decades earlier Dad had run into a childhood friend. He had 1 arm completely outlined. He said he wanted to be The Tattooed Man in the circus, but never went back for more. NOT CARNIE FOLK WORTHY!

Late one night a knock at the door. Dad said, "Go check that out." (thanks Dad)
2 couples, one more drunk than the other. Girl says, "All I want is a camera on my ankle." I asked her, "Any particular kind?" The other guy interrupts and says, "I just want your basic nuclear mushroom cloud." I closed the door.

Door is already locked. KNOCK KNOCK. "All I want is a date tattooed on my arm."
OK , Mistake! "What date?" I ask. He replies, "Tomorrow's." Buddy sketched it on him over and over for at least 20 minutes. We're about ready to throw him out...
a little bigger, fancier...on and on, and a couple of music notes too... Then he said, "Tomorrow is a big day for me. My dream comes true, I'm opening my music store." I congratulated him and asked where abouts. "I haven't decided yet" was his answer. From then on when I heard the expression "All I want is a..."
FORGET IT

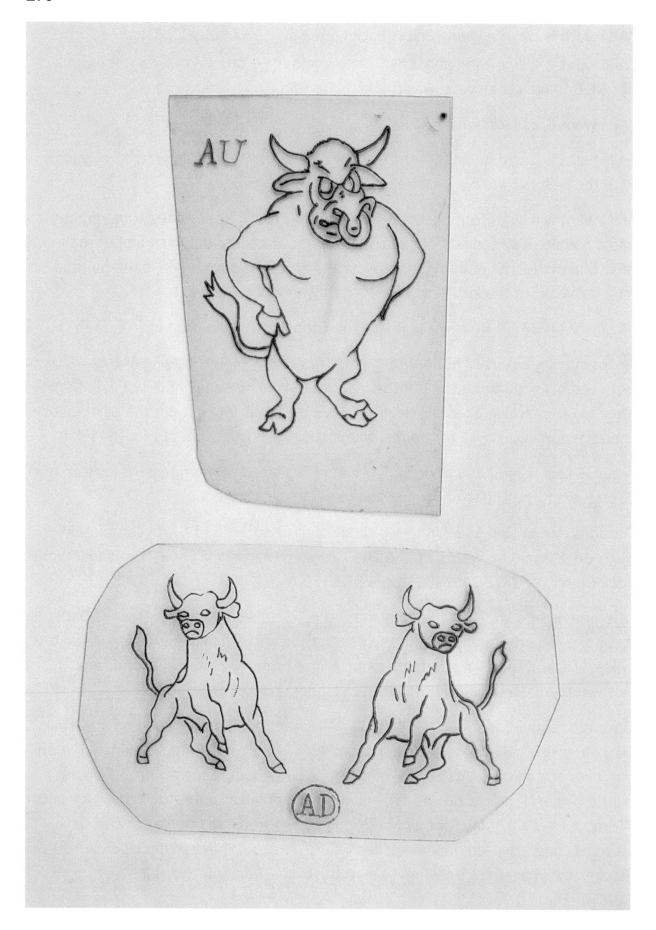

OUR FAVORITE STORIES: (Usually during a full moon)

Zodiac signs were really popular in the 1980's.
A guy points to the flash and says, "I'd like this bull."
Buddy asks, "Are you a Taurus?"
The guy says, "No, I'm a commercial fisherman."

The first Marine (well he said he was a Marine) I worked on looked very young. He was old enough and handed me a license. He was getting the Eagle, Globe and Anchor on his upper left arm. I noticed on the other arm, sticking out from the T-shirt sleeve, the end of a stem of a rose and " Mommi" below it. I start talking to him like he is 5. He then asks if I will add a bit more color to the rose on his right arm. He pulls up his sleeve to reveal the rest; Kill a Commi - for Mommi

I want "Lefty" tattooed on my right arm…

Two girls come in. One wants a Dingo and the other wants a clove of garlic!

*** I'm asking myself at what point do I stop using the term Girl and call females Ladies or Gals or ? I've also noticed repeatedly the references also made to weight. Fifty + years ago we were all obsessed by Twiggy, the bone thin English actress, model and singer. Airline stewardesses would regularly be put on a scale and fined or fired it they were over their contracted weight.

Young guy gets a tattoo on his lower gut. PROPERTY OF _____
He said he'll use a marker to write names in.

Caller: "I want to make an appointment for between 9 and 10 pm…well it's not for me it's for a friend of mine from out of town…" I ask for an idea of what he wants to get – Big or small. Answer: "Not too big. He's only here for a couple of days…"

Two nice girls – one has a Thumper tattoo. Couldn't help but notice it was done in blue! I couldn't tell what it was. Her girlfriend wants a cat face – like this - but - not really – well I want the cat face to have a possessed look. At that moment the phone rings, "How much to cover a Jesus tattoo?" We should have set him up with the possessed cat!

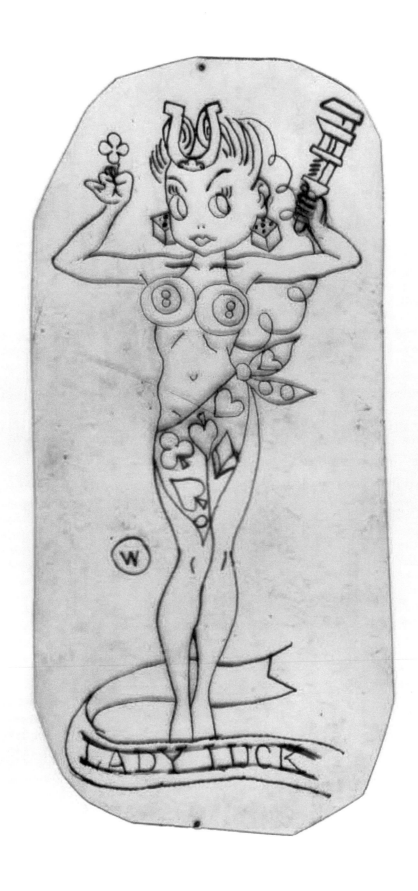

Bar code for a pack of 5 watt lightbulbs!

Yan from Belgium with very short hair only spoke French. He had some cash in his hand and wanted a small tattoo. He is checking his pockets for his ID. In the meantime I'm helping him sign in and I ask him if he is in the service, he says, "Oui" (Yes). I ask his address. "Mon maison est sur la mer." (My house is on the sea.) I ask the name of the ship he is stationed on and he says, "Lucky Lady". I said to him, "What kind of service are you in?" In his heavy accent he replied, "No Service. Touriste. Booze Cruise."

"When I win the Lotto, I'm comin' down for the whole Last Supper on my back."

A guy gets the Nike swoosh looking logo on his ankle. The second it's done he jumps up and starts running in extra slow motion all around the shop.

Buddy is sketching a picket fence above a girl's bikini line. She takes the pen from him 3 times & draws on herself. Buddy asks if she is going to give the pen back. Now she does the almost crying voice, "You're yelling at me..." We decide she's not getting anything. Next, a girl got a Bulldog with BITE ME written under it.

One night as the 11 p.m. local news was on TV, a guy looks up and said, "That's me!" WELL, Yes, it was! We missed the part about what he did and I didn't feel the need or have the courage to ask...

Two nights in a row! It's the same 2 young guys in the Navy from Alabama. They have strong southern accents, and they talk a lot! One tells us again he is engaged. Then he says he doesn't know if he's ready for marriage. "I don't love her." His friend asks, "How do you know?" Answer; "All I want to do is lick her navel." (Now we're therapists! Some nights tattooing is 60% art and 40% therapist).

"I want a blue rams head", said a customer to me. Then he asks me, "What's your sign?" (Old pick-up line). He then said, "You must do a lot of Zodiac signs. Did you know God is an Aries?" There were times Buddy would whisper to me, "Smile and take their money".

A man 40+ (at the time I was in my 20's. I guess 40+ to me then was lots older), his wife and their 6-year-old son – all well dressed and clean cut (more words used to describe in the 80's). The father pulls out a picture of the Holy Spirit, fire, doves, cross...very fancy. "I'd like this on my ass." Buddy replied, "NO WAY."

A skinny 18-year-old: "I want a big Tryadactyl on my right bicep."

A 27-year-old RN comes to get "Property of Clancy" on her behind...

Teacher about 30 years old: "I'd like to get a UFO engine." Dad asks if he brought a picture...

"I'M FIRST!" They're all drunk, almost a brawl – what do you want...The brawler says a peace sign! He holds up 2 fingers and says he wants it to look like his own hand, including the big cut he had on his thumb...! WOW

A drunk came in like he owned the place. Said, "I'm a Boston Cop and I've got $4,000. in my pocket. I want to go next." I explained that's not fair nor the way we do things. Then he turns to a kid he's never seen before and gives him 40 bucks and leaves.   Big Shot

A woman customer: "My son asked me to get a spider but I don't want to get a spider." I ask, "How old is your son?" Answer: "He's 5, don't make it too big."

Holy Saturday, the day before Easter, a real drunk comes in. I ask if he has an appointment and he answered yes. I ask him his name and he says, "Jesus." I wanted to say that can't be. You're dead until tomorrow morning. (So many things we didn't say out loud until we were cleaning up at the end of the night. One of us would say, "What about that guy..." as these notes were jotted down.)

A guy and his girlfriend: He is getting her name. She announces, "I'm 19 and he's 33. You know what's nice about going with an old man? We've been in 3 different bars tonight and I haven't been carded. Right Honey? I lived upstairs from him and his wife. He was my landlord. Right Honey? We were both living upstairs together and his wife threw us out last week." I said, "I would have thrown you out a long time ago." She looked at me surprised! They were talking about going to the beach together for the first time. He asked her, "do you like to walk...play frisbee,... etc." Her response, "NO! I go at 9 a.m. I bring a clock and turn every half hour til 4 p.m." He didn't seem thrilled. She called him HONEY so many times that when they were leaving both Dad and myself said, "Bye Honey." Perfect example of "money in the bank" making the name slightly larger at no extra charge, anticipating the bigger more expensive cover up. Honey did come back a few months later to have her name covered.

Newlyweds; Wife is getting his name. She says, "Honey, give me your hand." He says, "Squeeze the seat." !!!

We pull into the parking lot and a guy comes walking around the gas station towards us. He's dressed in old sheets and playing a flute. Dad says, "What the hell is that?" My answer, "Full moon. Want to go home?"

Wanna Bee; A guy comes in for a Marine Corps emblem. Two months later he comes in for the Navy emblem! He pulls off his shirt and we see 2 more, the Army and Coast Guard. He is actually in none of them! Try that in the Hell's Angels!

1986-ish The first 2 words about this in the notebook I kept said, "Full moon"...A guy and an overweight girl (said chubby in the notes) came in. She announces, my tattoo is spreading and faded. I got my butterfly in the late 60's...She drops the jeans to reveal very short terry cloth shorts (another 80's thing), knee high nylons (again 80's) lots of cellulite and white beaded moccasins. She points to her leg and is discussing the spreading tattoo. We look and look again. No tattoo! The next guy thru the door asks where the nearest strip joint is...

Pretty 18-year-old girl, wearing a local high school jersey, and her 17 year old boyfriend come in. He wants her to get a small tattoo on her ankle – ½ way thru she unclenches her teeth and her fists, looks at him and says, "Your ass is mine!" Nothing like a young girl who says what's on her mind. Later she asks Buddy how long has he been tattooing. His reply was 39 years. She responds, "Do you like it?"

The night Dad made Superman cry... Guy was only getting the **S** on the front of his hip, only an inch high.

A 'lady' walks in wearing a leather vest, already has a grim reaper tattooed on her arm, gray stringy hair and is wearing a big pin on her vest that says, "FUCK OFF SHITHEAD." In a very soft-spoken voice (which surprised me) she wanted to ask me a question – but- it's getting late and by the outfit and the pin starring me in the eye, I'm all set. This was the end of another hot, full moon, summer weekend. I suggested maybe if she hurries, she can catch the shop up the street still open. Away she went! There were nights that worked and nights when the other shop would play the same game sending their unwelcomed down to us...

"Will sunscreen smudge my tattoo?"

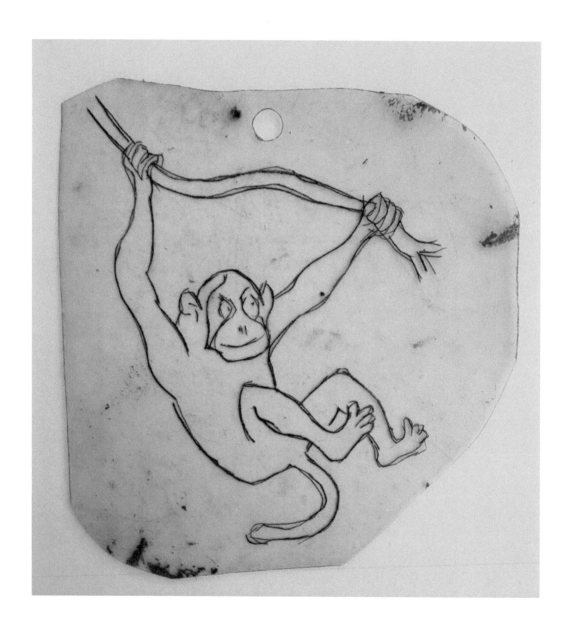

Some nights if a potential customer already had too much to drink, we'd suggest they go and get a coffee. Sometimes Buddy would say, "keep walking you'll find it". Most times they didn't come back or couldn't find their way back. Yeah!

Back in the day, every T-shirt had a tag on the back. A guy said he would be coming back for a tag on the back of his neck, "Made in USA"...and he did.

A gal was getting MMM tattooed on her. She told us it stood for, "Marsha, Marsha, Marsha like on the Brady Bunch." Her name was Judy.

A gal said she liked my job. She told me her dream job is to name nail polishes.

A cow with lettering: "MOOGARITAVILLE".

Another cow tattoo: "I want to get a small cow tattooed on the front of my hip, small." She's brought her own picture. We make the stencil, tattoo it on... She announces she doesn't like it and is almost in tears. Someone in the shop suggests putting red boots on it. We do and she LOVED it!

A 19-year-old girl comes in with her 3-year-old son to get a recently done name covered. She told us what she wanted by saying, "I was a-thinkin' in my head"... (If you're going to think it's a great place to start.)

A girl with a slight accent is at the shop with her husband. We asked where she is from and she told us originally Newfoundland. While he is getting his tattoo we're all talking about the beautiful scenery in and around Newfoundland. I am looking at the girl as I say, "I spent my honeymoon up in your area." The guy jumps in "You went to Raynham?" (45 minutes up the road)

The night we stopped for a sandwich and ordered a BLT. The waitress asked, "Do you want lettuce and tomato on that?" Is there a size above full moon?

A male nurse wants: "A bull with blue balls."

TMI: Peroxide head gal feels the need to tell me, "My lover has blond pubies..."

The guy that got the monkey on his back is back. It's about a year later. "I got to get that monkey off my back. Cover it, and I don't care with what." (Again, we're here to please and thanks for the entertainment).

Half a dozen sailors in the Italian Navy come in wearing dress whites. They speak no English. One almost passes out. I ask, "Do you want a drink of water?" Another pulls out the English translation dictionary. Buddy says, "Aqua?" His face lights up.

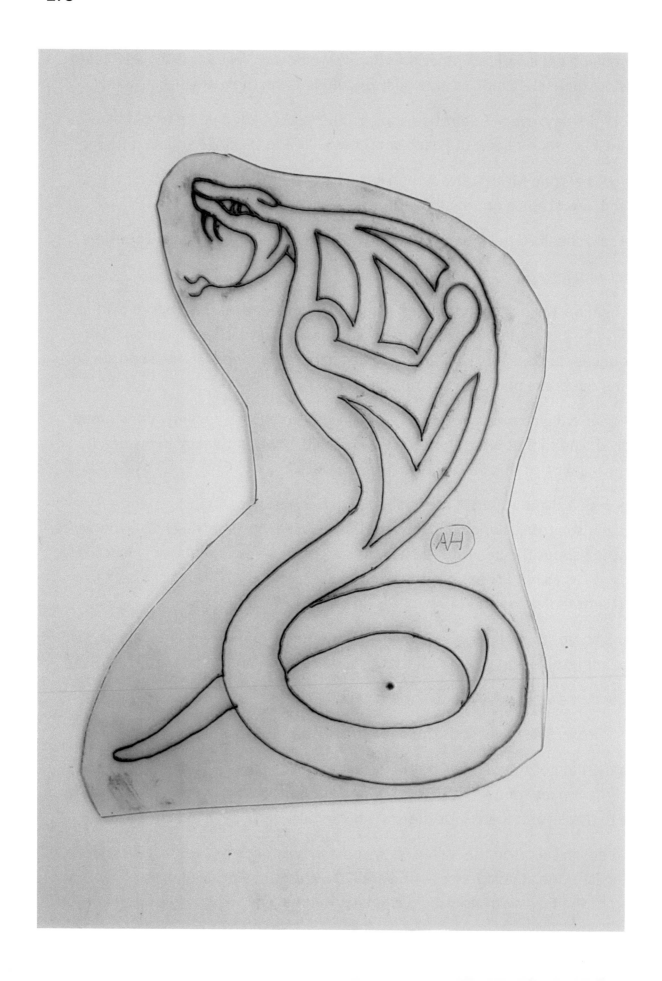

Another customer in the shop suggests Vino. "AHHH Vino" he said. A girl speaks up and tells us she can help the three undecided sailors pick out a tattoo. She turns to them, pokes one in the arm, curls the fingers up Italian style and says, "Whicha one?" Well, one decides on an eagle with an American Flag and an American shield. Another gets: "Death Before Dishonor" written in English. These guys have all been in the Italian navy for 6 or 7 years each!

"Can you close the mouth of that cobra so he'll look nicer?"

Guy in a wheel chair with MD gets: "There's no need to fear, Underdog is here."

Girls with electric blue spike shoes are artists...OR so this gal tells me. She is holding a notebook with a picture of a Pegasus drawn with unusual proportions. She insists on getting her design exact – I make the acetate stencil and then it's a little big, so I shrink it some more... Her friend is also an artist and a sculptor! She shows us a picture she has drawn – it looks like a leaf. I'm about to pour some green to color the leaf and she says, "Will you make the feather brown and yellow?" In this case, A + B = A very full moon!

"I want to get a tattoo of my boa... it's in the car..." *And that's a good place for it!*

A guy comes in, "I'd like a Guinee -T." I have no idea what he wants. Then he points to the tank top for sale. "I'm from Joursey."

A guy married for 2 months had to call his wife to find out how to spell her name! As he is being worked on an 18-year-old blond gal comes in to ask a few questions about getting a rose on her ankle. He (the newly-wed) tries to convince her to get it on her breast and is offering to pay if he can watch. **PIG**

PLACEMENT:

During a routine mammogram the technician pointed out I had a small dark spot on my chest (it was another freckle). She said since I have a tattoo on my shoulder, it was tattoo ink that travelled to the front. She had no idea I tattooed for a living. All I could think of was a person going to sleep with a cartoon character tatttooed on the right arm and waking up with it on the leg. I laughed to myself and didn't bother to educate her. That was my last trip to that facility.

More difficult: Customers who had lost a lot of weight - or - an older person with little elasticity left of the skin. At some point the flying eagle on the neck could droop down looking like it was about to crash. The left hand stretching the skin is working at least 3 times harder than the hand with the machine in it.

A skinny sailor took off his shirt. Buddy said, "Where'd you go?" Then he insisted on a good-sized eagle on his upper arm. Dad said the wings touched at the back of the arm. That's what he really wanted...another happy customer!

A guy wanted a tattoo of a woman's face on his chest. He pulled off his shirt and Buddy said, "Put your shirt back on." He was so hairy the pretty woman would have looked like the Bearded Lady in the circus.

A New England guy (let's call him Joe G.) carefully planned the placement of his tattoo. The Colts logo on the outer forearm but upside down. (Most of us New Englanders are Patriots fans.) I of course ask, why upside down. In one motion he showed me that when he raises his arm to give the finger to Patriots fans, you know he's a Colts' fan. <u>Goodnuff</u> explanation for me. (Turns out that's his last name!)

APPRECIATION DAY:

In 2014 we had a Buddy Mott Appreciation Day at Battleship Cove in Fall River, Massachusetts. I thought the 2 guys who came up with the idea were nuts. Buddy had a stroke almost 2 years before that. He for the most

part did have a strong recovery and his tattoo story telling came back! Sunday afternoons became a thing, hanging out with him at the Veteran's Home where he stayed for care. Corey Goyette from Inflicting Ink in Portsmouth, RI and The Fall River Tattoo Company in Fall River, MA, Ken Johnson (KJ) who owned Federal Hill Tattoo in Providence, RI and a top notch tattoo machine builder, my sister, nephew Leander and myself would all be entertained.

I admit it took a while to talk me into having the event. Turns out it wasn't good, it was GREAT! We invited some of our old customers, relatives and friends. Rusty, at that time had retired from tattooing and had some medical issues of his own, said to my father, "Buddy, I want to thank you for giving me a great life" followed by a hug. I'm thrilled I had the opportunity to witness that and enjoyed the outpouring of love and stories that afternoon. Justin Lim, a well-known sign painter, was in town from Indiana and painted this beautiful sign during the event.

Bob Ames also came attended. I dragged him up in front of the crowd so we could all see his large back tattoo. Buddy always said it was one of his favorites, an eagle, a pretty

woman with a rose and the lettering (like the stencil on the cover) "THOSE WHO DARE WIN". Bob also designed a tattoo that, on purpose, will never be finished. It is a tattoo of Buddy's hand using his rotary machine, starting the outline of a panther.

The night of Buddy's 80th birthday party, Bob asked to have his tattoo signed with a tattoo. Of course.

Over the years my favorite stories are the ones where fellow artists tell of their younger years walking into the shop for the first time and having Buddy make such an impression that they decided to start perusing tattooing as a career. A guy from Mass. told us he and his friends, after going to RI the 1st time, wanted to go back the next weekend but they couldn't get a ride so they stole a car! When cleaning out the countless sign in cards stored in the rafters of Dad's cellar at home, I looked for the date KJ (mentioned earlier) would have turned 18 and found it! He had told us meeting

Buddy was his introduction and inspiration to learn the craft. 2015, Carolyn & I took a road trip to Mooncusser Tattoo in Provincetown, MA, located on the tip of Cape Cod. We decided to surprise KJ with his original sign in card. He and a group of tattoo artists were finishing up their week-long guest artist spots. We also met up with the owner Khristian, who had also been to our Newport shop. Then we were invited to their final dinner with the group followed by a boat ride to watch the sunset. Artist Anxious Dave brought us to the boat and off we all went. I was noticing we got lots of looks... it was a beautiful good sized power boat. As I got off, I noticed the name of the boat in large letters on both sides; The Sea Word. Recently I heard The Sea Word sank! There is a new boat, (Khristian's new baby) named, The Sea Section.

THE NIGHT WE BROKE THE RULES:

2007 and Buddy's tattooing was still on target but his legs were starting to give out. One night the boys and my sister were also at the shop hanging with Grandpa. Leander, Carolyn's son, was showing a drawing of lettering he made of his own initials. LJLJ surprisingly in the traditional Old English font, not the graffiti styles he is known for. My son Zack pulled out a drawing he made of a nautical star. There were also 2 banners through it. They read: "BUDDY" "MOTT". The boys said someday they would like to get their drawings tattooed. I suggested

we make stencils just to see how they would look on. I then asked my Dad if he wanted to put the tattoos on. He said quickly, "No way! There not old enough!" Leander & Zack were only a few months shy of 18. I told him I didn't think they would arrest and convict an 83-year-old man, with no record, for tattooing his two Grandsons. I'm thrilled he did them that night. It was the best night all around! Leander also asked his Grandpa to tattoo his signature below the initials. He gladly obliged. Buddy then retired.

Recently my nephew, Leander, got a couple of new tattoos. He went to see his friend Andrew Monroe, that he went to school with, who works at Fortune Tattoo in Newport. My sister and I got invited along. I asked Andrew if I could do some of the coloring in the tiger for old times' sake. He didn't hesitate and said, "YES". Leander looked surprised! My precalculated thought of bringing Andrew a gift of an old panther head stencil, to let me have a turn, wasn't necessary but was much appreciated. Keep in mind I still do have my license but hadn't tattooed since 2009. Yes, it all came back so quickly even though the machine was heavy and the tube was huge but WOW that was a great time! I wanted my sister to do some coloring on her son too. She was thinking about it and I found myself doing my version of a scene from the movie Rocky. The one where Mickey, Rocky's trainer, is giving him words of encouragement. I said to her using a raspy voice, "Come on kid, put the gloves on and jump back in the chair" and she did.

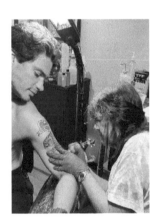

Writing this book has given me the opportunity to remember many great moments, contact and rekindle friendships, and tell stories to new friends.

 I would also like to thank my husband Alan for his love and support on the journey. He has 3 tattoos. A Guardian Angel holding a sword (on his shoulder), a US ARMY tattoo and one for the Hattie Dawg. He became caregiver for the pup after his best friend Paul passed away at age 40.

Also, many thanks to Zack, my relatives and good friends for encouraging me to write the book Buddy often talked about doing. Recently when I mentioned to my son, I was thinking about trying to forge aluminum, he said, "Good idea, right after you finish the book".

This is where the shop was and what you would drive by today (note arrow). I've seen a minivan parked in the spot with just a little bit of room to spare.

Hard to believe that small space provided so many years fun and stories.

All the researching and writing throughout these pages, trying to figure out the actual addresses of his shops and I recently came across this from 1971:

No address necessary!

...and (1962) who the hell is
"Sailor Al"??!! Allen was Buddy's middle name. Nineteen cents of sales tax due for the month, could have been from engraving sales?

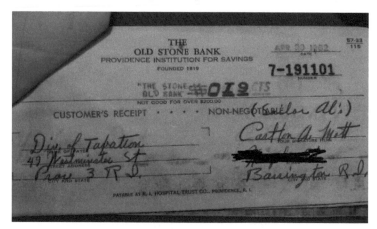

This is what I designed for the family gravestone. A traditional tattoo of a cross, rose and heart. (The small G Clef hanging from the banner is for Mom's musical career). Of course, it wouldn't be complete without a pair of sparrows on the top corners.

His funeral was done with Military Honors. After the Funeral Director concluded the service, no one was surprised when we pulled Buddy's favorite cannon (the one with the 12" barrel and 1" bore) out of the trunk and fired it.

The Warren Monument Company was wonderful, patiently working with me. I was invited to come and watch the etching process and then they gave me the honor of pulling off the stenciling paper.

Tattoo artists will go to gravesites and make a rubbing of a fellow artist's stone. Pictured are Corey Goyette, Danny Vasquez and Bruce Deslauriers.

Buddy's stone is located in Colt's Park at the North Burial Ground, Bristol, Rhode Island. The last cemetery entrance on the right before the bike path, a block up on the left.

Buddy didn't have thank you tattooed on his knuckles, that's only him playing with a Sharpie marker again, as he was telling us of some artists that had "PAY ME" tattooed on the open palm of the hand. He said he didn't feel the need to do that. Instead, you got a sincere thank you from him as you paid. If a guy handed him every bill in his wallet, Buddy would hand one back saying, "I'm not going to take your last buck, I've been there."

We did manage to communicate, by acting out stuff, with the customers that didn't speak English. When the tattoo was complete and the customer was paying, he would surprise them by saying: "Thank you" in their language. Buddy had taught himself the phrase *Thank you* in well over a dozen languages.

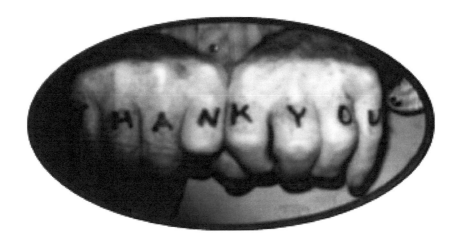

"Good night Maggie"...

188

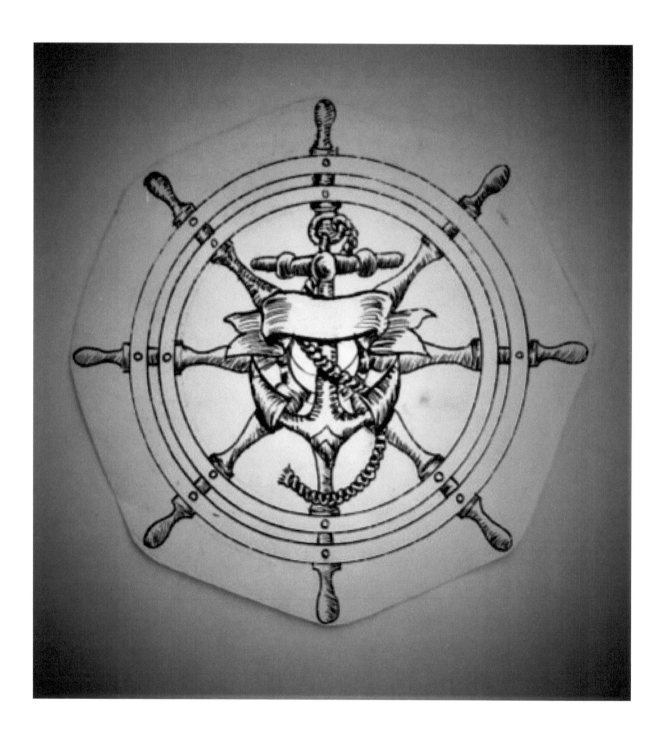

Buddy Mott
Newport, R.I.
1963

A portion of the proceeds from the sale of every book is being donated to the Rhode Island Veteran's Home in Bristol. This is where Buddy spent his last year and a half being well cared for.

Contact info:

Instagram: Marilyn_Mott_Tolleson

Email: buddystattooshop@gmail.com

Check out:
ebay.com/usr/buddystattooshopping

Offering for sale: Homeward Bound canvas prints and Buddy's pastel ship prints on canvas ready to hang, acetate stencils, bumper stickers and more.

Printed in the USA
CPSIA information can be obtained
at www.ICGtesting.com
LVHW071947011123
762649LV00019B/783